SMALL-BATCH SNACKING CAKE COOKBOOK

SMALL-BATCH
Snacking Cake
COOKBOOK

75 Quick-Prep Recipes
to Satisfy Your Sweet Tooth

Aimee Broussard

Photography by Marija Vidal

ROCKRIDGE
PRESS

For general information on our other products and services or to obtain technical support, please contact our Customer Care Department within the United States at (866) 744-2665, or outside the United States at (510) 253-0500.

Rockridge Press publishes its books in a variety of electronic and print formats. Some content that appears in print may not be available in electronic books, and vice versa.

Interior and Cover Designer: Jenny Paredes
Art Producer: Janice Ackerman
Editor: Anne Goldberg
Production Editor: Melissa Edeburn
Production Manager: Martin Worthington

Photography: ©2021 Marija Vidal. Food styling by Stéphane Réau.

Author Photo: Courtesy of TahJah Harmony.

Paperback ISBN: 978-1-63878-602-3
eBook ISBN: 978-1-63878-292-6
R0

{ To Brian, for making life
infinitely sweeter }

Contents

◇◇◇◇◇◇◇◇◇◇◇◇◇◇◇◇◇◇

Introduction

◇◇◇◇◇◇◇◇◇◇◇◇◇◇◇◇◇◇◇◇◇◇◇◇◇◇◇◇◇◇◇◇◇◇◇

I can trace the source of my unwavering sweet tooth–the kitchen of my great-grandmother, Eleanor–in great detail. I can see her, donning a handmade apron and sauntering over with a homemade biscuit and teacup of "coffee milk" (equal parts coffee, milk, and sugar). I, meanwhile–eyes as big as saucers, seated at attention, feet dangling above the floor they would take years to reach–giggled excitedly in anticipation of enjoying my very own grown-up drink.

It was the milk and sugar for me.

I've switched to café au lait, but I now know that I can combine milk, sugar, flour, and a few other ingredients to make my biggest love: cake. I have even gone so far as to develop a recipe for Café au Lait Breakfast Cake (page 24)–you'll find it in the Cake for Breakfast chapter, because if I'm going to take you down memory lane, I might as well make a cake for the journey.

Sometime in 2014 I was introduced to the concept of a no-occasion cake. My friend Katie contributed her mama's "best-ever" recipe for Chocolate Chip Snack Cake to my Traveling Apron Recipe Swap–this crazy project I created to blog about a hand-made apron and empty recipe binder I sent on a cross-country trip to collect recipes.

The recipe was delightful, but I was more intrigued by the concept, novel to me, of a "snacking cake"–a cake created not for any particular occasion or celebration, but just for the pleasure of eating it. Katie's mom, Debbie, wins all the accolades, having let her daughter eat cake as an after-school snack, but considering you're reading this book, you, my friend, also have a prize: 75 ways to celebrate the everyday with snacking cake.

The beauty of the small-batch snacking cake recipes found among these pages is that they are uncomplicated and unfussy, often mixed in a single bowl, and ready quickly, so your craving for something sweet can be satisfied with minimal effort. And not surprisingly, small-batch means the pans you'll be using will be small: 8- or 9-inch square or round pans or regular-size loaf pans, providing just enough cake to satisfy your craving but not so much cake that it goes stale.

The recipes are big on flavor and mostly make use of ingredients the well-stocked, cake-loving baker will already have on hand. Cake for everyone anytime! You'll see that snacking cake squares are perfect for grab-and-go breakfast, after-school snacking, and birthday celebrations. They are the sort of cakes that can brighten a friend's day, welcome a new neighbor, and sweetly congratulate the new mom whose oven is the last thing on her mind.

My sincerest hope is that these recipes find a place in your heart and home and that they bring smiles to all who enjoy them. So when you're ready, I invite you along on my snacking train. Consider me the cake conductor who will lead you straight to temptation town with the flip of these pages. All aboard!

CHAPTER ONE

The Small-Batch Snacking Cake Kitchen

The small-batch snacking cake kitchen describes a well-equipped and sufficiently stocked kitchen that allows you to appease your desire for cake at a moment's notice with minimal effort and mess and in minimal time. In this book, you won't find hard-to-obtain ingredients. You won't find ingredients called for only in a single recipe. And you won't need to purchase fancy baking pans. In fact, you may have everything you need to bake some of these recipes at this very moment.

Equipping Your Kitchen for Small-Batch Cakes

There is nothing quite as frustrating as having a sudden urge to bake a cake, only to realize that you are out of cocoa powder or don't have the required baking pan. I've been there. It's not fun. This chapter discusses basic equipment, handy tools, and ingredients you should always have on hand before you even think about hitting the preheat button on the oven. It also discusses substitutions and ingredient hacks if you run into problems and going to the store is not an option.

THE BAKEWARE

You'll find that my preferred pan is 8 inches, but all recipes can be made in a 9-inch pan if that's what you already have and want to use. When using a larger pan, you'll just need to anticipate a shorter baking time and increase the oven temperature by 25°F to allow for the larger surface area. Be sure your pans are at least 2 inches deep. I generally use basic light-colored aluminum pans because cakes made in aluminum pans bake in less time than in pans made of other materials. I find aluminum also yields the most consistent results. If glass or ceramic pans are what you have, use them. The following baking pans will be needed for the recipes in this book:

8- or 9-inch square baking pan: This is the pan I suggest most frequently. In my opinion, the 8-inch square pan is the most ideal pan for creating perfectly snack-able squares of cake, and allows for a higher rise.

8- or 9-inch cast-iron skillet: There are only a couple of recipes that use a cast-iron skillet. It's not entirely necessary, but it does allow for the most delightfully crisp chocolate chip cookie cake edges if you're looking to add a new pan to your arsenal.

8- or 9-inch round cake pan: Similar to the 8-inch square pan, for these scaled-down recipes I prefer the higher rise you get from the smaller, 8-inch round cake pan, but a 9-inch round cake pan can be used if that's what you have.

Loaf pan: I'll be using an 8½-by-4½ loaf pan for all the loaf cake recipes. A 9-by-5-inch pan can also be used, though your cake will be thinner, and the baking time will be shorter than the times indicated in the recipe using the smaller pan. A loaf pan with a nonstick coating is desirable.

SUBSTITUTING PANS

I believe an 8-inch square baking pan is optimal for snacking cakes, but when you want a traditional-looking slice of cake (hello, birthdays!), reach for a round pan. The 8-inch square pan and the 8-inch round pan can be used interchangeably. A 9-inch square or round pan can also be used, but know that it will result in a thinner cake, and the baking times will be a bit shorter. A general guideline when substituting a larger pan for a smaller one is to check on the cake 10 minutes earlier than the bake time listed in the recipe. Glass or ceramic pans can be substituted for my preferred aluminum pan.

THE TOOLS

Here are a few basic tools you'll want to have on hand to make snacking cake baking as seamless as possible:

Mixing bowls: My go-to for a single batch of cake batter is a 4- or 5-quart bowl. Bowls that are a little smaller work well for preparing toppings.

Measuring cups: You'll want to have two types of measuring cups in your arsenal—one for dry ingredients and one for liquids. For dry ingredients, I have a favorite set of metal measuring cups (yes, I just admitted out loud I have a favorite set of measuring cups) that magnetically nestle into one another. A 2-cup measure will also come in handy for the dry ingredients if you don't have one of those already. For liquids, a 1-cup spouted glass measuring cup is good for measuring as well as pouring ingredients without spilling.

Measuring spoons: These are for measuring small quantities of ingredients like baking soda, baking powder, and salt, or when extra precision is required.

Electric mixer: While some of the one-bowl recipes can be mixed by hand, an electric mixer, whether it be a handheld or stand mixer, will come in quite handy for creaming butter or preparing frostings.

Whisk: A whisk with sturdy wires will be useful for mixing together glazes.

Wooden spoon: A wooden spoon can be used if you do not have a mixer. It will take much longer to incorporate the ingredients, but if it was good enough for my great-grandmother, then it'll work in a pinch for you, too.

Rubber/silicone spatula: A flexible spatula is necessary for mixing and transferring ingredients, as well as scraping down the bowl.

Mini offset spatula: This tool is optional but useful for spreading the top of cake batter smooth before baking, as well as spreading frosting and glaze.

Nonstick baking spray: I believe so strongly in nonstick baking spray with flour (I use Baker's Joy brand) that I've included it here as a necessary tool to have on hand. If you like making life difficult for yourself, you may use regular butter and flour to line your pans.

Parchment paper: Parchment paper for me is the insurance policy of cake baking. You can certainly try your odds with a well-greased pan, but lining the pan with parchment will never fail you. Use the parchment paper in combination with nonstick baking spray and thank me later.

The majority of recipes will instruct you to make a parchment paper sling, which allows for easy and clean cake removal every time. To create a sling, cut a sheet of parchment that is as just as wide as your pan in one direction and much longer in the other direction. Place it inside the pan, letting the excess paper hang over two opposite edges. The overhanging paper now becomes your handles, giving you something to hold onto when removing the cake from the pan and transferring it to the wire rack to cool.

Wire rack: A wire rack is useful for cooling your cakes, keeping them off your countertops and allowing air to circulate.

Fine-mesh sieve/sifter: This tool is handy for dusting powdered sugar over finished cakes.

Zester: Many recipes call for a bit of citrus zest, and a zester is much easier to use than a box grater. It can also be used for chocolate shavings (as well as a host of savory applications, not that we care as much about those), so it's a worthwhile purchase if you don't already have one.

Oven thermometer: I say you need this because I recently had my relatively new double ovens serviced only to learn that they were registering at 325°F, though set for 350°F. I now keep an oven thermometer in my oven at all times to double-check the true temperature. Ovens vary, and this inexpensive gadget keeps you on track.

Stocking Your Kitchen for Emergency Cake Cravings

In my close circle of friends, we have someone known for dropping off frozen cocktails when things are not going as planned and yet another friend who is known to show up curbside with cake and disposable forks in hand to sweeten up a bad day. Of the two, you can probably guess which friend I am.

When emergencies call for cake, I'm able to act quickly because of a well-stocked kitchen, and in this section I'll teach you my ways so that you, too, can handle any emergent needs for cake that come your way.

PANTRY

The recipes in this book use basic, everyday ingredients in order to satisfy your craving for cake quickly and easily. The following list will give you an idea of what I keep on hand and will prepare you for making most recipes in this book.

Flour: I use unbleached all-purpose flour in the majority of these recipes. For the special diets chapter, I used a gluten-free alternative flour. I like Bob's Red Mill Gluten Free 1-to-1 Baking Flour because it includes xanthan gum, which is necessary for binding the ingredients together.

Should you elect to use a different brand of gluten-free flour, you'll need to add 1 teaspoon of xanthan gum in order for these recipes to work.

Sugars: Granulated sugar, powdered sugar, and light brown sugar will be necessary for these recipes. I also keep turbinado sugar on hand. Turbinado is a coarse, raw sugar great for sprinkling over baked goods like scones and cookies and can be used on top of the breakfast loaf cakes for an added sweet crunch.

Leaveners: Baking soda and baking powder will be used frequently in these recipes to help cakes rise beautifully. Both need to be as fresh as possible, which you can easily test:

For baking soda: Add 1 teaspoon of baking soda to ¼ cup of distilled white vinegar; it should bubble and fizz. If not, head to the store for a replacement.

For baking powder: Spoon 1 teaspoon of baking powder into a heatproof container and pour ¼ cup of boiling water on top. You want to see it bubble and fizz.

Spices: My favorite spices are ground cinnamon, nutmeg, cloves, and ginger. To ensure that spices stay fresh, purchase them in small quantities. Spices should be used within six months of purchase, so I usually do a seasonal update.

Cocoa powder: These recipes call for unsweetened Dutch process cocoa. Dutch process cocoa has been treated with alkali to lower its acidity, making for a dark color and milder flavor.

Chocolate: Dark, semisweet, milk, and white chocolate are all friends of mine. It doesn't really matter if the chocolate is in bar form or chips, as long as the quality is there. For a special-occasion cake, I may reach for a higher-end chocolate, but for the most part, the readily available brands at the grocery store will work just fine.

Oil: Neutral-tasting vegetable oil works best in most of these recipes; I like canola. I also like coconut oil in some of the family favorite recipes that once used shortening.

Maple syrup: It's a little bit pricier, but you want to look for pure maple syrup for baking.

Molasses: Molasses has a good shelf life and won't break the bank to purchase. You'll need it in the fall when Ginger-bread Cake (page 113) is a must.

Honey: Honey is an ingredient I splurge on, always buying local, and I encourage you to do the same. Don't throw out honey that has crystallized. It occurs when the natural sugars in honey bind together.

Peanut butter: I skip anything that contains artificial sweeteners like xylitol and stick with the creamy classics like Skippy or Jif. Natural and organic can certainly be used, just be sure to stir, stir, stir the oil that collects at the top before adding it to recipes calling for peanut butter. It will affect both taste and liquid content otherwise.

Vanilla: Vanilla extract will be used a lot in these recipes, so go ahead and buy the large bottle. And don't be too concerned about the difference between pure vanilla extract and artificial vanilla extract, which is much cheaper. *Cook's Illustrated* performed a double-blind study on the top 10 best-selling vanilla extract products in the country and found that when used in baking, artificial vanilla yielded as satisfying a flavor as its more expensive competitors.

Dried fruit: Dried fruit makes a great topping and provides extra texture to recipes. Be sure to look for dried fruit that is still moist and plump as it provides the most flavor for your cakes. I find the best selection in the bulk bins at the specialty health-centric grocers.

Nuts: I've yet to meet a nut I didn't like, though my nut of choice is the pecan, likely because I grew up picking (and eating) them with my grandmother. The two nuts most commonly used in these recipes are pecans and walnuts. Storing nuts in the freezer will allow them to retain their freshness longer.

WHOLE-GRAIN OPTIONS

The majority of the recipes contained in this book are based on using unbleached all-purpose flour for convenience, but for added flavor and health benefits, occasionally adding whole wheat flour to cake batters, especially the ones with chocolate chips, or including oats in the crumb toppings will add both texture and nutrients to your baked goods. To use whole wheat flour in baking, replace no more than 25 percent of the all-purpose flour with whole wheat flour for the best texture and flavor.

REFRIGERATOR

Eggs: Always use large eggs at room temperature. I know some will debate that eggs from the fridge will work just fine, but ever since I took a baking class at the Louisiana Culinary Institute, it has been ingrained in my head that room-temperature eggs provide maximum volume when whipped and will distribute more evenly throughout batters.

Milk: Whole milk is preferred, but many of these recipes were tested with 2 percent, and it can be used as well. I wouldn't go any lower than 2 percent though, as fat-free milk may affect the liquid content. Vegan recipes were tested with canned coconut milk as a dairy milk alternative and canned coconut cream for the vegan whipped cream.

Buttermilk: Buttermilk adds a bit of tang to recipes and is commonly found in older recipes, likely due to its longevity when refrigerated. I use it frequently because of the tender texture it provides to cakes.

Sour cream: Sour cream adds texture, moisture, and flavor to cakes, so I use the full-fat option. The reduced-fat and fat-free versions just don't work the same way.

Cream: Heavy (whipping) cream will be used for whipped topping. Don't try to substitute half-and-half for heavy cream, as it won't whip.

Butter: All of the recipes in this book call for unsalted (sometimes called sweet) butter. However, at home, I've used both unsalted and salted butter and can rarely tell the difference. If salted is what you prefer or have on hand, just omit any added salt from the recipe.

Frozen fruit: I prefer to bake with fresh fruit, but you just can't control when a craving insists on something out of season. In those cases, frozen fruit is a great alternative. First rinse the fruit to keep the colors from bleeding, then blot with a paper towel and toss with a bit of flour to keep the fruit from sinking in the batter.

INGREDIENT HACKS AND SUBSTITUTIONS

Forgot to take out the eggs? Quickly bring cold eggs to room temperature by submerging them in a bowl of hot (but not boiling) water.

Honey crystallized? Bring honey back to life by placing the jar in a hot water bath for a few minutes. The crystals will melt like magic.

Brown sugar turned rock hard? Place it in a microwave-safe bowl and lay a damp paper towel over it. Microwave for about 20 seconds. You can prevent this from even happening by placing a slice of bread in the same airtight storage container with the sugar to keep it soft.

No time for softening butter? Butter typically takes about an hour to reach room temperature, but you can also cut the butter into small sections and microwave in short bursts of 5 to 10 seconds. Butter is softened enough when an indentation remains when you press it. If you've zapped it too long in the microwave, just stick it in the fridge for a bit to firm it back up.

No sour cream? I use sour cream in most of my recipes because of the flavor and moisture it provides, but if you have Greek yogurt on hand, use that. Just be sure it's the whole-milk kind.

Bananas not quite ripe? Place unpeeled bananas on a baking sheet lined with parchment paper or aluminum foil to catch any leakage. Bake for 30 minutes at 300°F, allow to cool, then proceed with perfectly mashable bananas.

Cake Making Basics

You've heard the phrase "fake it till you make it," but I'm going to need you to semi-forget about that while we discuss cake baking. While the concept of quick-and-easy, scaled-down recipes for perfect little snacking cakes seems simple enough, there is still some attention to detail required to ensure that the cake that comes out of the oven is the same one you've envisioned in your head.

READ THE RECIPE

It seems elementary, but before you get too excited and start measuring ingredients, read the recipe in its entirety. There's nothing worse than having a heated oven cranking only to realize you're missing a key ingredient.

PREHEAT OVEN

Once you've read the recipe, make sure your oven rack is set in the center of the oven, set the oven to the required temperature, and preheat it. Allowing batter to sit while waiting for the oven to come to temperature often results in a sunken cake, so you want your oven to have a sufficient head start before you start mixing. Ideally, give your oven an extra 10 to 15 minutes at its optimal baking temperature so that the oven surfaces are also hot and compensate for heat escaping when you open the oven to place your pan inside.

GET ORGANIZED

Set out all ingredients in their proper measurements and at their proper temperatures before getting started. Check your leavening to ensure it is still fresh (see page 5) if you haven't purchased it recently. Once it's added to the batter, there's no turning back.

PAN PREP

Greasing your baking pans properly ensures that the cake or loaf comes out in one piece. I spray the pans with nonstick baking spray with flour and then use a piece of parchment paper. For round pans, a round of parchment placed in the bottom does the trick. For square pans and loaf pans, create a parchment paper sling by using a strip long enough to extend past the edge of the pan on two opposite sides. This creates two handles that will allow for easy lifting from the pan.

MIXING 101

Do you know how some recipe authors will include DO NOT OVERMIX! in their recipes, all capitalized with an exclamation point for emphasis, almost like they're yelling at you? I won't yell, but I will explain why you should listen when instructed to mix until "just combined." Mixing until just combined means you are mixing just until you can no longer see any traces of flour in the batter. Continuing to mix beyond this point allows gluten to develop and results in a weak cake with unfavorable taste and texture. Besides making the cake gummy and chewy, do you know what else happens to weak cakes? They collapse.

PAN PLACEMENT

Place your pans on the center rack of the oven to ensure even heat distribution and baking.

CHECKING FOR DONENESS

My great-grandmother would always say "your nose knows" when explaining how she knew when cakes were done, but I'm not my great-grandmother, so I use a combination of visual cues and the good ole toothpick inserted in the center coming out mostly clean method to go along with my sniffing abilities. I say "mostly clean" because often if your toothpick comes out completely dry, your cake may also be dry. A few moist crumbs is ideal, but you don't want any wet batter. A cake is considered done when it is puffed up and the edges have begun to pull away from the sides of the pan; lighter-colored batters will also be golden.

COOLING

Cooling methods vary from cake to cake, but most of the cakes will head to a wire rack to cool enough to be handled safely (about 15 minutes), then transferred from pan to rack to cool completely. A few of the more delicate cakes, however, will need to cool completely in the pan before being handled. Allowing the cakes to cool on a rack is ideal because it allows air to circulate around the cake, keeping the crunchy edges, especially on loaf cakes.

FINISHING

My personal mantra is that you are never fully dressed without jewelry, and that applies to cakes without toppings. With that being said, you'll find that these recipes are packed with flavor on their own and can be enjoyed either without accessories or with a minimal dusting of powdered sugar. Should you want to kick things up a notch, I've included suggested toppings for each. You'll want to wait until the cake is fully cooled before adding frosting.

STORAGE

Based on the small size of these snacking cakes, I'm betting you won't have a need to store beyond a couple of days, but leftover cake should be covered with plastic wrap or aluminum foil and stored at room temperature.

HIGH-ALTITUDE BAKING

The higher the altitude, the lower the air pressure, which means cakes take longer to bake and liquids evaporate faster; therefore, some adjustments likely need to be made. A good starting point is to increase your oven temperature by 10°F and decrease the baking time by 5 to 8 minutes. This gives the cake a chance to bake more rapidly and set before it dries out. You'll also need to make some ingredient adjustments—less leavening and flour, additional liquids, etc.—based on just how high your elevation is. There are helpful guides online that you can use to calculate these adjustments based on your altitude. My favorite is found on the King Arthur Baking website.

About the Recipes

I have given great thought to providing you with snacking cake recipes that will satisfy just about every possible cake craving you may have . . . and satisfy it quickly! And while these cakes are quick to whip up, don't let that lead you to believe they are unimpressive. You control whether cakes straight out of the oven are your jam, just as they are, or if you're feeling spunky and decide to get creative with their "jewelry," i.e., toppings and presentation. I've offered some suggestions in the "Top it off" tips, but feel free to make adjustments based on your personal preferences.

These recipes were all developed with quick snacking in mind, but they also hold their own as entertaining or gift-giving options. Their small size makes them ideal for baking up several recipes, mixing and matching the toppings found in the final chapter, and having an array of cake square options rather than an excess of all the same flavor.

And if you were thinking that's where the endearment stops, you'd be wrong. They make for the most delightful homemade gift! I've used these snack cakes for everything from welcoming a new neighbor, to gifting a friend when they've been under the weather, to consoling a family member after the loss of a loved one.

But maybe it's only about you and your own snacking satisfaction needs. You are in good company and my kind of person. You will find the recipes in this book are simply organized by main flavors, occasion, or dietary requirements, allowing you to locate something to satisfy your craving both quickly and easily. And the icing on the cake is the finale ending with more than a dozen ways to do just that.

Glazed Honey Bun Cake ◆ Page 16

Cake for Breakfast

Oatmeal Cake

♦ MAKES 1 (8-INCH) SQUARE CAKE ♦

This incredibly light and fluffy snack cake is a nice twist on actually having oatmeal for breakfast. The oats in the batter make it a little more substantial for those mornings when your sweet tooth takes priority but you still need to make it to lunch!

PREP TIME: 15 minutes ♦ **BAKE TIME:** 45 minutes ♦ **SERVINGS:** 9

Nonstick baking spray (with flour)
1 cup quick-cooking oats
1 cup boiling water
1 cup all-purpose flour
1 teaspoon baking soda
½ teaspoon ground cinnamon

¼ teaspoon salt
⅛ teaspoon ground nutmeg
8 tablespoons (1 stick) unsalted butter, at room temperature
½ cup granulated sugar

½ cup packed light brown sugar
2 teaspoons vanilla extract
1 teaspoon maple extract
2 large eggs
¾ cup mini chocolate chips

1. Preheat the oven to 350°F. Mist an 8-inch square baking pan with baking spray and line with a parchment sling (see page 9).

2. In a small heatproof bowl, combine the oats and boiling water and stir until the water is mostly absorbed. Set aside.

3. In a large bowl, combine the flour, baking soda, cinnamon, salt, and nutmeg. Set aside.

4. In a medium bowl, using an electric mixer on medium speed, cream the butter and granulated and brown sugars together for 2 to 3 minutes, until light and fluffy. Beat in the vanilla and maple extracts, then add the eggs, one at a time, beating just until each egg is incorporated.

5. Add the flour mixture to the butter-sugar mixture and beat on medium speed, just until the flour is worked into the batter. Add the oatmeal and beat until evenly distributed in the batter. Fold in the chocolate chips.

6. Scrape the batter into the prepared baking pan. Bake for 40 to 45 minutes, until a toothpick inserted in the center of the cake comes out mostly clean.

7. Transfer the pan to a wire rack to cool completely. Remove the cake from the pan, discard the parchment, and cut into 9 squares to serve.

STORAGE: Will keep tightly covered with plastic wrap or in an airtight container at room temperature for 4 to 5 days.

TOP IT OFF: For extra maple flavor, drizzle the cooled cake with Maple Glaze (page 129).

Glazed Honey Bun Cake

This delicious yellow cake with a streak of cinnamon in the middle and a cinnamon glaze on top turns a classic convenience store treat into a snacking cake. One taste and I'm betting you'll never buy store-bought again.

PREP TIME: 15 minutes ◆ **BAKE TIME:** 30 to 35 minutes ◆ **SERVINGS:** 9

FOR THE STREUSEL
- ½ cup packed light brown sugar
- 1 teaspoon ground cinnamon
- ½ teaspoon ground nutmeg

FOR THE CAKE
- Nonstick baking spray (with flour)
- 1 cup all-purpose flour
- 1 teaspoon baking powder
- ¼ teaspoon salt
- ¾ cup granulated sugar
- 4 tablespoons (½ stick) unsalted butter, at room temperature
- ¼ cup coconut oil
- ½ cup sour cream
- 1 teaspoon vanilla extract
- 2 large eggs

1. **Make the streusel:** In a small bowl, combine the brown sugar, cinnamon, and nutmeg. Set aside.

2. **Make the cake:** Preheat the oven to 350°F. Mist an 8-inch square baking pan with baking spray and line with a parchment sling (see page 9).

3. In a medium bowl, whisk together the flour, baking powder, and salt.

4. In a large bowl, using an electric mixer on medium speed, cream together the granulated sugar, butter, and oil for 2 to 3 minutes, until light and fluffy. Add the sour cream and vanilla and mix for another minute.

5. Add the eggs, one at a time, beating just until each egg is incorporated.

6. Add the flour mixture to the butter-sugar mixture a little at a time, mixing until just combined.

7. Pour half of the batter into the prepared baking pan, then sprinkle the streusel mixture on top. Scrape in the remaining batter and spread on top of the streusel. Bake for 30 to 35 minutes, until a toothpick inserted in the center of the cake comes out mostly clean.

8. Transfer the pan to a wire rack to cool completely. Remove the cake from the pan, discard the parchment, and cut into 9 squares to serve.

TOP IT OFF: While the cake is still warm, prick holes in the top of the cake with a skewer or fork and pour Cinnamon Glaze (page 129) over the top of the cake to complete the glazed honey bun effect.

Maple Cream Cake

◆ MAKES 1 (8-INCH) SQUARE CAKE ◆

This super-moist maple-flavored cake is perfect with morning coffee or afternoon tea. You can skip the maple frosting if you want, but it really enhances the cake with rich maple flavor.

PREP TIME: 15 minutes ◆ **BAKE TIME:** 25 to 30 minutes ◆ **SERVINGS:** 9

FOR THE CAKE

Nonstick baking spray (with flour)

8 tablespoons (1 stick) unsalted butter, at room temperature

1 cup granulated sugar

½ cup sour cream

1 large egg

½ cup maple syrup

½ teaspoon baking powder

1 cup all-purpose flour

FOR THE FROSTING

½ cup powdered sugar

2 tablespoons unsalted butter, at room temperature

1½ tablespoons maple syrup

½ teaspoon ground cinnamon

1. **Make the cake:** Preheat the oven to 350°F. Mist an 8-inch square baking pan with baking spray and line with a parchment sling (see page 9).

2. In a large bowl, using an electric mixer on medium speed, cream the butter and granulated sugar together for 2 to 3 minutes, until light and fluffy. Add the sour cream and egg, mixing until just combined. Add the maple syrup and mix to combine.

3. Add the baking powder and mix. Add the flour, a little at a time, mixing well after each addition, until just combined.

4. Scrape the batter into the prepared baking pan. Bake for 25 to 30 minutes, until a toothpick inserted in the center of the cake comes out mostly clean.

5. **Meanwhile, make the frosting:** In a small bowl, mix together the powdered sugar, butter, maple syrup, and cinnamon until smooth. Add more syrup if the frosting is stiff. It should be soft enough to spread smoothly.

6. Transfer the cake to a wire rack to cool for 10 minutes in the pan. Remove from the pan, discard the parchment paper, and set the cake right-side up on a serving plate.

7. Frost the top of the still-warm cake, then let cool completely. Make sure the frosting is set before cutting it into 9 squares.

Birthday Morning Yellow Cake

◆ MAKES 1 (8-INCH) ROUND CAKE ◆

I know that seeing a classic birthday cake in a breakfast chapter is unexpected, but have you ever been served birthday cake for breakfast? It's the best way to kick off a celebration of YOU! Topped with chocolate buttercream and sprinkles? Yes, please.

PREP TIME: 15 minutes ◆ **BAKE TIME:** 25 to 30 minutes ◆ **SERVINGS:** 8

Nonstick baking spray
(with flour)
1½ cups all-purpose flour
1 teaspoon
baking powder
½ teaspoon baking soda

¼ teaspoon salt
½ cup sugar
6 tablespoons (¾ stick)
unsalted butter, at room
temperature
1 large egg

1 teaspoon vanilla extract
⅓ cup buttermilk
Small-Batch Chocolate
Buttercream (page 133)
Sprinkles, for decorating

1. Preheat the oven to 350°F. Mist an 8-inch round cake pan with baking spray and line the bottom with a round of parchment paper.

2. In a medium bowl, whisk together the flour, baking powder, baking soda, and salt.

3. In a large bowl, using an electric mixer on medium speed, cream together the sugar and butter for 2 to 3 minutes, until light and fluffy. Add the egg and vanilla, mixing until just combined.

4. Add the flour mixture to the butter-sugar mixture, a little at a time and alternating with the buttermilk, mixing well after each addition, until just combined.

5. Scrape the batter into the prepared baking pan. Bake for 25 to 30 minutes, until a toothpick inserted in the center of the cake comes out mostly clean.

6. Transfer the cake to a wire rack to cool for 10 minutes in the pan. Remove from the pan and let the cake cool completely on the wire rack. Once cooled, discard the parchment and frost the cake (don't forget the festive sprinkles!). Cut the cake into 8 slices to serve.

Classic Sour Cream Coffee Cake

◆ MAKES 1 (8-INCH) SQUARE CAKE ◆

A sour cream coffee cake recipe is an essential piece of the snacking cake arsenal. This scaled-down version of my grandmother's prize-winning recipe is perfect for solo coffee time. One taste and you'll see why it was a hit.

PREP TIME: 15 minutes ◆ **BAKE TIME:** 35 to 40 minutes ◆ **SERVINGS:** 9

FOR THE TOPPING
1 cup chopped pecans
½ cup packed light brown sugar
1 teaspoon ground cinnamon

FOR THE CAKE
Nonstick baking spray (with flour)
8 tablespoons (1 stick) unsalted butter, at room temperature
½ cup granulated sugar

1 large egg
½ cup sour cream
½ teaspoon vanilla extract
1 cup all-purpose flour
½ teaspoon baking powder
½ teaspoon baking soda

1. Preheat the oven to 350°F. Mist an 8-inch square baking pan with baking spray and line with a parchment sling (see page 9).

2. **Make the topping:** In a small bowl, combine the pecans, brown sugar, and cinnamon together. Set aside.

3. **Make the cake:** In a large bowl, using an electric mixer on medium speed, cream together the butter and granulated sugar for 2 to 3 minutes, until light and fluffy. Add the egg and mix well. Add the sour cream and vanilla and mix to combine.

4. In a separate bowl, whisk together the flour, baking powder, and baking soda. Add the flour mixture to the butter-sugar mixture, beating until just combined.

5. Pour half of the batter into the prepared baking pan. Sprinkle half of the topping mixture on top of the batter. Cover with the remaining batter and finish with the rest of the topping mixture. Bake for 35 to 40 minutes, until a toothpick inserted in the center of the cake comes out with few crumbs clinging to it.

6. Transfer the cake to a wire rack to cool for 10 minutes in the pan. Remove from the pan and set on the wire rack to cool completely. Discard the parchment and cut the cake into 9 squares to serve.

Applesauce and Brown Sugar Crumb Cake

◆ MAKES 1 (8-INCH) SQUARE CAKE ◆

This cake is perfect for fall with its warm spices and cozy vibe. Add the optional walnuts to the crumb streusel for an over-the-top applesauce cake, perfect with coffee. This snack cake also extends beyond breakfast and is perfectly portable for an afternoon hayride.

PREP TIME: 15 minutes ◆ **BAKE TIME:** 30 to 35 minutes ◆ **SERVINGS:** 9

FOR THE STREUSEL
½ cup all-purpose flour
½ cup chopped walnuts (optional)
¼ cup packed light brown sugar
2 tablespoons unsalted butter, at room temperature

FOR THE CAKE
Nonstick baking spray (with flour)
1½ cups all-purpose flour
½ teaspoon baking soda
½ teaspoon ground cinnamon
¼ teaspoon ground cloves
¼ teaspoon ground nutmeg

¼ teaspoon salt
4 tablespoons (½ stick) unsalted butter, at room temperature
¾ cup packed light brown sugar
½ cup sweetened applesauce
½ teaspoon vanilla extract
2 large eggs

1. **Make the streusel:** In a small bowl, combine the flour, walnuts (if using), brown sugar, and butter. Using two forks, work the ingredients together just until combined.

2. **Make the cake:** Preheat the oven to 350°F. Mist an 8-inch square baking pan with baking spray and line with a parchment sling (see page 9).

3. In a medium bowl, combine the flour, baking soda, cinnamon, cloves, nutmeg, and salt until the spices are evenly distributed. Set aside.

4. In a large bowl, using an electric mixer on medium speed, cream the butter and brown sugar together for 2 to 3 minutes, until light and fluffy. Beat in the applesauce until combined. Add the vanilla and the eggs, one at a time, beating until each egg is incorporated.

5. Add the flour mixture to the butter-sugar mixture, a little at a time, and beat just until combined.

6. Scrape the batter into the prepared baking pan and sprinkle with the streusel. Bake for 30 to 35 minutes, until a toothpick inserted in the center of the cake comes out mostly clean.

7. Transfer the pan to a wire rack to cool completely. Remove the cake from the pan, discard the parchment, and cut into 9 squares to serve.

Café au Lait Breakfast Cake

Café au lait is coffee with hot milk added to it. I've been enjoying this combo since I was a youngster, when my first taste of this classic pair set off my lifelong love affair with all things cream and sugar. This delicious snack cake proves you can have your coffee and eat it, too.

PREP TIME: 15 minutes ◆ **BAKE TIME:** 30 to 40 minutes ◆ **SERVINGS:** 9

Nonstick baking spray (with flour)

8 tablespoons (1 stick) unsalted butter, at room temperature

¾ cup sugar

2 large eggs

1 teaspoon vanilla extract

1½ cups all-purpose flour

1 teaspoon baking powder

½ teaspoon salt

⅓ cup half-and-half

3 tablespoons brewed espresso or very strong black coffee

1. Preheat the oven to 350°F. Mist an 8-inch square baking pan with baking spray and line with a parchment sling (see page 9).

2. In a large bowl, using an electric mixer on medium speed, cream the butter and sugar together for 2 to 3 minutes, until light and fluffy. Add the eggs, one at a time, beating just until each egg is incorporated. Beat in the vanilla.

3. In a medium bowl, whisk together the flour, baking powder, and salt.

4. In a measuring cup, combine the half-and-half and espresso.

5. Add the flour mixture to the butter-sugar mixture, a little at a time and alternating with the cream-espresso mixture, mixing well after each addition, until just combined.

6. Scrape the batter into the prepared baking pan. Bake for 30 to 40 minutes, until a toothpick inserted in the center of the cake comes out mostly clean.

7. Transfer the cake to a wire rack to cool for 10 minutes in the pan. Remove from the pan and set on the wire rack to cool completely. Discard the parchment and cut the cake into 9 squares to serve.

TOP IT OFF: Cream Cheese Glaze (page 127) is a wonderful addition here and really rounds out the cream portion of this coffee-and-cream cake. Prick holes with a skewer or fork into the top of the still-warm cake (still in the pan) before glazing to allow some of the glaze to seep into the cake.

VARIATION: Stir 1 cup of lightly toasted walnuts into the batter just before baking to bring a subtle nuttiness and a bit of crunch to this cake.

Honey Yogurt Upside-Down Granola Cake

◆ MAKES 1 (8-INCH) SQUARE CAKE ◆

Tired of boring ole yogurt with granola for breakfast? Never had an upside-down cake that didn't include pineapple? This no-fruit-added twist on a traditional breakfast combination is sure to beat the Monday morning blues with its sweet and crunchy granola topping. After all, what is granola if not a pre-baked oat streusel?

PREP TIME: 15 minutes ◆ **BAKE TIME:** 30 minutes ◆ **SERVINGS:** 9

Nonstick baking spray (with flour)

8 tablespoons (1 stick) unsalted butter, at room temperature, divided

½ cup granola

⅓ cup packed light brown sugar

½ cup granulated sugar

1 large egg

¾ cup whole-milk Greek yogurt

¼ cup honey

1 teaspoon vanilla extract

1½ cups all-purpose flour

½ teaspoon baking soda

¼ teaspoon salt

1. Preheat the oven to 350°F. Mist an 8-inch square baking pan with baking spray.

2. Place 4 tablespoons of butter in the prepared baking pan and place in the oven for 5 minutes, or until the butter melts. Remove the pan from the oven.

3. In a small bowl, combine the granola and brown sugar. Spread evenly over the melted butter.

4. In a large bowl, using an electric mixer on medium speed, cream the remaining 4 tablespoons of butter and granulated sugar together for 2 to 3 minutes, until light and fluffy. Add the egg and combine well. Add the yogurt, honey, and vanilla and mix until well combined.

5. In a medium bowl, whisk together the flour, baking soda, and salt. Add the flour mixture to the yogurt mixture, a little at a time, and beat just until combined.

6. Scrape the batter over the granola mixture in the baking pan. Bake for 30 minutes, or until a toothpick inserted in the center of the cake comes out mostly clean.

7. Transfer the cake to a wire rack to cool for 10 minutes in the pan. Loosen the cake from the sides of pan and invert onto a serving plate (so the bottom is on top) to cool completely. Transfer any granola stuck in the pan on top of the cake. Cut the cake into 9 squares to serve.

Raspberry Layer Breakfast Cake

◆ MAKES 1 (8½-BY-4½-INCH) LOAF ◆

This sweet butter cake layered with jam is moist, dense, and better than a thumbprint cookie. I've used raspberry here, but the options are limitless.

PREP TIME: 15 minutes ◆ **BAKE TIME:** 1 hour ◆ **SERVINGS:** 8

Nonstick baking spray (with flour)

8 tablespoons (1 stick) unsalted butter, at room temperature

1 cup sugar

2 large eggs, at room temperature

½ cup sour cream

1 teaspoon vanilla extract

½ teaspoon almond extract

2 cups all-purpose flour

1 tablespoon baking powder

½ teaspoon salt

½ cup raspberry jam or preserves

1. Preheat the oven to 350°F. Mist an 8½-by-4½-inch loaf pan with baking spray and line the pan with a parchment sling (see page 9), with the overhang on the long sides.

2. In a large bowl, using an electric mixer on medium speed, cream the butter and sugar together for 2 to 3 minutes, until light and fluffy. Add the eggs, one at a time, beating just until each egg is incorporated. Add the sour cream, vanilla, and almond extracts, beating until well combined.

3. In a large bowl, whisk together the flour, baking powder, and salt.

4. Add the flour mixture to the butter-sugar mixture, a little at a time, mixing just until combined.

5. Spoon one-third of the batter into the prepared loaf pan. Top the batter with ¼ cup of raspberry jam, followed by another layer of batter, then the remaining ¼ cup of raspberry jam. Finish with the remaining batter. Bake for 55 minutes to 1 hour 10 minutes, until a toothpick inserted in the center of the cake comes out mostly clean.

6. Transfer the cake to a wire rack to cool completely. Remove from the pan, discard the parchment, and cut into 8 slices to serve.

Breakfast Cereal Coffee Cake

This cake turns the flavors and texture of your favorite breakfast cereal into a portable treat! Because of the honey in the batter, this cake works best with the suggested Cheerios, but you could use any cereal that doesn't have a fruity or chocolate flavor.

PREP TIME: 15 minutes ◆ **BAKE TIME:** 30 minutes ◆ **SERVINGS:** 9

Nonstick baking spray (with flour)

1½ cups all-purpose flour

1 teaspoon baking powder

½ teaspoon baking soda

4 tablespoons (½ stick) unsalted butter, at room temperature

½ cup packed light brown sugar

2 large eggs

1 cup whole milk

1 teaspoon vanilla extract

¼ cup honey

1½ cups Honey Nut Cheerios cereal, divided

1. Preheat the oven to 350°F. Mist an 8-inch square baking pan with baking spray and line with a parchment sling (see page 9).

2. In a large bowl, combine the flour, baking powder, and baking soda.

3. In a large bowl, using an electric mixer on medium speed, cream the butter and brown sugar together for 2 to 3 minutes, until light and fluffy. Add the eggs, one at a time, beating just until each egg is incorporated. Beat in the milk, vanilla, and honey.

4. Add the flour mixture to the butter-sugar mixture, a little at a time, mixing just until combined. Fold in 1 cup of cereal.

5. Scrape the batter into the prepared baking pan. Cover the top of the batter with the remaining ½ cup of cereal. Bake for 25 to 30 minutes, until a toothpick inserted in the center of the cake comes out mostly clean.

6. Transfer the cake to a wire rack to cool completely. Remove from the pan, discard the parchment, and cut into 9 squares to serve.

Olive Oil Cake with Honey Simple Syrup

◆ MAKES 1 (9-INCH) ROUND CAKE ◆

In her sorority cookbook from the 1970s, my grandmother has dog-eared an olive oil cake recipe and written only the word "excellent" next to it. I've taken the liberty of modernizing the recipe and earning a "!" to go along with that "excellent" review. The volume of this batter is slightly larger than for the other recipes in this book, so make sure to use a 9-inch, rather than an 8-inch pan.

PREP TIME: 15 minutes ◆ BAKE TIME: 35 minutes ◆ SERVINGS: 8

FOR THE CAKE
Nonstick baking spray
  (with flour)
¾ cup honey
½ cup sugar
3 large eggs
1½ cups extra-virgin
  olive oil
1½ cups whole milk

2 teaspoons grated
  lemon zest
2 teaspoons fresh
  lemon juice
2 cups all-purpose flour
1 teaspoon
  baking powder
½ teaspoon salt

FOR THE HONEY SYRUP
½ cup honey
½ cup sugar
½ cup water

1. **Make the cake:** Preheat the oven to 350°F. Mist a 9-inch round cake pan with baking spray. (I don't line the pan for this cake, but if you want to be extra safe, you can add a round of parchment.)

2. In a large bowl, using an electric mixer on medium speed, beat the honey, sugar, and eggs together until well combined. Add the oil, milk, lemon zest, and lemon juice and mix well.

3. In a medium bowl, whisk together the flour, baking powder, and salt. Add the flour mixture to the wet cake batter, mixing until just combined.

4. Scrape the batter into the prepared pan. Bake for about 35 minutes, or until a toothpick inserted in the center of the cake comes out mostly clean.

5. Transfer the cake to a wire rack to cool for 15 minutes in the pan. Loosen the sides of the cake and set right-side up on a serving plate to cool completely.

6. **Make the honey syrup:** In a small saucepan, combine the honey, sugar, and water. Bring to a simmer over medium-high heat, stirring to dissolve the sugar, and simmer for about 10 minutes, or until the liquid reduces and is as thick as a light syrup. Remove the pan from the heat and allow to cool to room temperature.

7. Prick holes in the top of the cake with a skewer or fork. Top the cooled cake with the honey syrup, allowing the syrup to seep into the holes. Cut the cake into 8 slices to serve.

TOP IT OFF: A dollop of Homemade Whipped Cream (page 130) pairs wonderfully with this cake.

VARIATION: Instead of the honey syrup and pricking holes into the cake, dust with a light coating of powdered sugar.

Cinnamon Sugar Doughnut Cake

◆ MAKES 1 (8-INCH) ROUND CAKE ◆

At my house, the weekend calls for doughnuts. This snackable cake makes for a fun take on this weekly tradition, and tastes just like an oversize baked cinnamon-sugar doughnut. You won't even have to change out of your pajamas.

PREP TIME: 15 minutes ◆ **BAKE TIME:** 30 minutes ◆ **SERVINGS:** 8

FOR THE CAKE
Nonstick baking spray
  (with flour)
1½ cups all-purpose flour
1 teaspoon
  baking powder
½ teaspoon baking soda
1 teaspoon ground
  cinnamon

¼ teaspoon salt
½ cup packed light
  brown sugar
½ cup whole milk
1 large egg
2 tablespoons unsalted
  butter, melted
1 teaspoon vanilla extract

FOR THE TOPPING
½ cup granulated sugar
1 teaspoon ground
  cinnamon
4 tablespoons (½ stick)
  unsalted butter, melted

1. **Make the cake:** Preheat the oven to 350°F. Mist an 8-inch round cake pan with baking spray and line the bottom with a round of parchment paper.

2. In a medium bowl, whisk together the flour, baking powder, baking soda, cinnamon, and salt. Set aside.

3. In a large bowl, using an electric mixer on medium speed, whisk together the brown sugar, milk, and egg until well combined. Add the melted butter and vanilla.

4. Add the flour mixture to the egg-milk mixture, a little at a time, and blend until just combined.

5. Scrape the batter into the prepared baking pan. Bake for 30 minutes, or until a toothpick inserted in the center of the cake comes out mostly clean.

6. Transfer the cake to a wire rack to cool for 10 minutes in the pan. Remove from the pan and set on the wire rack to cool completely. Discard the parchment.

7. **Make the topping:** In a small bowl, combine the granulated sugar and cinnamon. Use a pastry brush to coat the top of the cake lightly with the melted butter, then sprinkle with the cinnamon sugar.

8. Cut the cake into 8 slices to serve.

VARIATION: Once the cake is cool enough to handle, use an oversize cookie cutter to cut out the center of the cake, to resemble an oversize doughnut.

Pumpkin Spice Latte Cake

◆ MAKES 1 (8-INCH) SQUARE CAKE ◆

Imagine the rich, warming flavors of your favorite fall latte being whipped together into a handheld, snack-size treat. If you're thinking to yourself how lovely that would be, then you are in luck because that's exactly what I have done. I once served these little guys at a tailgate thinking they might be passed over for brownies, and I'll have you know they were the first to disappear! Make this one at the first sign of crunchy leaves.

PREP TIME: 20 minutes ◆ **BAKE TIME:** 30 minutes ◆ **SERVINGS:** 9

Nonstick baking spray (with flour)

2 cups all-purpose flour

1 teaspoon baking powder

½ teaspoon baking soda

½ teaspoon salt

2 teaspoons ground cinnamon

½ teaspoon ground ginger

½ teaspoon ground nutmeg

¼ teaspoon ground allspice

8 tablespoons (1 stick) unsalted butter, at room temperature

¾ cup granulated sugar

¼ cup packed light brown sugar

¼ cup vegetable oil

1 teaspoon vanilla extract

2 large eggs

1 cup canned unsweetened pumpkin puree (not pumpkin pie filling)

1. Preheat the oven to 350°F. Mist an 8-inch square baking pan with baking spray and line with a parchment sling (see page 9).

2. In a medium bowl, whisk together the flour, baking powder, baking soda, salt, cinnamon, ginger, nutmeg, and allspice. Set aside.

3. In a large bowl, using an electric mixer on medium speed, cream the butter and both sugars together for 2 to 3 minutes, until light and fluffy. Beat in the oil and vanilla. Add the eggs, one at a time, beating just until each egg is incorporated. Beat in the pumpkin puree until fully combined.

4. Add the flour mixture to the butter-sugar mixture, a little at a time, mixing well after each addition, until just combined.

5. Scrape the batter into the prepared baking pan. Bake for about 30 minutes, or until a toothpick inserted in the center of the cake comes out mostly clean.

6. Transfer the pan to a wire rack to cool completely. Remove the cake from the pan, discard the parchment, and cut into 9 squares to serve.

TOP IT OFF: A latte is often topped with whipped cream, so I suggest serving a dollop of Homemade Whipped Cream (page 130) with this cake. Cream Cheese Glaze (page 127) is also an excellent pairing.

Blueberry Skillet Cake • Page 57

Apple Fritter Loaf Cake

◆ MAKES 1 (8½-BY-4½-INCH) LOAF CAKE ◆

If you like apple fritters, you'll love this cake. It tastes just like its eponymous treat, but is leaps and bounds easier to whip together when a craving hits.

PREP TIME: 15 minutes ◆ **BAKE TIME:** 1 hour 5 minutes ◆ **SERVINGS:** 8

Nonstick baking spray
   (with flour)
⅓ cup packed light
   brown sugar
3½ teaspoons ground
   cinnamon, divided
1½ cups all-purpose flour

1 teaspoon
   baking powder
1 teaspoon baking soda
¼ teaspoon salt
¾ cup plus 3 tablespoons
   granulated sugar

8 tablespoons (1 stick)
   unsalted butter, at room
   temperature
2 teaspoons vanilla extract
2 large eggs
½ cup buttermilk
1¾ cups chopped peeled
   baking apples

1. Preheat the oven to 350°F. Mist an 8½-by-4½-inch loaf pan with baking spray and line the pan with a parchment sling (see page 9), with the overhang on the long sides.

2. In a small bowl, combine the brown sugar and 2 teaspoons of cinnamon. In a medium bowl, combine the flour, baking powder, baking soda, and salt. Set both bowls aside.

3. In a large bowl, using an electric mixer on medium speed, cream ¾ cup of granulated sugar and the butter together for 2 to 3 minutes, until light and fluffy. Beat in the vanilla, then add the eggs, one at a time, beating just until each egg is incorporated.

4. Add the flour mixture to the butter-sugar mixture, a little at a time and alternating with the buttermilk, mixing well after each addition, until just combined.

5. In another medium bowl, combine the remaining 3 tablespoons of granulated sugar and 1½ teaspoons of cinnamon. Add the apples and toss until the apples are coated with the cinnamon sugar.

6. Scrape half of the batter into the prepared loaf pan. Add half of the apples in a layer and gently push them down into the batter. Sprinkle half of the brown sugar–cinnamon mixture over the apples. Repeat, adding the remaining batter, apples, and brown sugar–cinnamon mixture. Use a skewer to swirl it all together. Bake for 1 hour to 1 hour 5 minutes, until a toothpick inserted in the center of the cake comes out mostly clean.

7. Transfer the pan to a wire rack to cool completely. Remove the cake from the pan, discard the parchment, and cut into 8 slices to serve.

STORAGE: Will keep tightly covered with plastic wrap or in an airtight container at room temperature for 4 to 5 days.

TOP IT OFF: This is especially delicious when drizzled with Cream Cheese Glaze (page 127).

Banana Cream Cheese Loaf Cake

◆ MAKES 1 (8½-BY-4½-INCH) LOAF CAKE ◆

In this updated twist on classic banana bread, swirls of cream cheese provide a creamy, tangy counterpoint. This cake is sure to become a new favorite or perhaps even replace your go-to banana bread recipe.

PREP TIME: 20 minutes ◆ **BAKE TIME:** 1 hour 20 minutes ◆ **SERVINGS:** 8

Nonstick baking spray (with flour)

FOR THE CREAM CHEESE LAYER

1 (8-ounce) package cream cheese, at room temperature
½ cup granulated sugar
1 large egg

1 teaspoon vanilla extract
1 tablespoon all-purpose flour

FOR THE CAKE

¾ cup mashed ripe bananas (about 2 bananas)
¾ cup packed light brown sugar

⅓ cup unsalted butter, melted
⅓ cup sour cream
2 large eggs
2 teaspoons vanilla extract
1½ cups all-purpose flour
½ teaspoon baking soda
¼ teaspoon baking powder
¼ teaspoon salt

1. Preheat the oven to 350°F. Mist an 8½-by-4½-inch loaf pan with baking spray and line the pan with a parchment sling (see page 9), with the overhang on the long sides.

2. **Make the cream cheese layer:** In a medium bowl, using an electric mixer on medium speed, beat the cream cheese and granulated sugar together until creamy. Add the egg and vanilla and beat until combined. Add the flour and beat just until it's worked into the batter. Set aside.

3. **Make the cake:** In a large bowl, using an electric mixer on medium speed, beat the bananas, brown sugar, and melted butter together until combined. Beat in the sour cream, eggs, and vanilla until fully incorporated.

4. In a medium bowl, combine the flour, baking soda, baking powder, and salt. Add the flour mixture to the banana mixture and beat on medium speed, just until the flour is incorporated.

5. Pour half of the batter into the prepared loaf pan. Dollop the cream cheese mixture over the top of the banana batter. Gently spread it out to cover any spots of batter still showing through. Pour the remaining banana batter on top of the cream cheese layer. Spread it out to cover the cream cheese layer. Use a butter knife or skewer to gently swirl the cream cheese layer and banana batter together.

6. Bake for 1 hour 15 minutes to 1 hour 20 minutes, until a toothpick inserted in the center of the cake comes out mostly clean.

7. Transfer the pan to a wire rack to cool completely. Remove the cake from the pan, discard the parchment, and cut into 8 slices to serve.

STORAGE: Will keep tightly covered with plastic wrap or in an airtight container at room temperature for 3 to 4 days.

TOP IT OFF: Double up on the cream cheese and top this with Cream Cheese Glaze (page 127).

Lemon Poppy Seed Loaf Cake

• MAKES 1 (8½-BY-4½-INCH) LOAF CAKE •

Sweet-and-tart sets this cake apart, making it perfect for summer celebrations or anytime you need an afternoon snack with a bit of pucker.

PREP TIME: 15 minutes • **BAKE TIME:** 1 hour 10 minutes • **SERVINGS:** 8

Nonstick baking spray
 (with flour)
1 cup sugar
½ cup vegetable oil
2 large eggs

1 cup sour cream
1 tablespoon grated
 lemon zest
¼ cup fresh lemon juice
1 teaspoon vanilla extract

1¾ cups all-purpose flour
¼ cup poppy seeds
2 teaspoons
 baking powder
¼ teaspoon salt

1. Preheat the oven to 350°F. Mist an 8½-by-4½-inch loaf pan with baking spray and line the pan with a parchment sling (see page 9), with the overhang on the long sides.

2. In a large bowl, using an electric mixer on medium speed, beat the sugar and oil together until combined. Add the eggs, sour cream, lemon zest, lemon juice, and vanilla and beat just until the eggs are incorporated.

3. In a medium bowl, combine the flour, poppy seeds, baking powder, and salt. Add the flour mixture to the sour cream mixture and beat on medium, just until the flour is worked into the batter.

4. Scrape the batter into the prepared loaf pan. Bake for 1 hour to 1 hour 10 minutes, until a toothpick inserted in the center of the cake comes out mostly clean.

5. Transfer the pan to a wire rack to cool completely. Remove the cake from the pan, discard the parchment, and cut into 8 slices to serve.

STORAGE: Will keep tightly covered with plastic wrap or in an airtight container at room temperature for 4 to 5 days.

TOP IT OFF: Lemon Glaze (page 129) ramps up the zing and really takes this cake over the top.

Cherry Chocolate Chip Loaf Cake

◆ MAKES 1 (8½-BY-4-INCH) LOAF CAKE ◆

The addition of cherries to this traditional chocolate chip combination keeps this cake from being anything but traditional. It's like a cherry cola, but in snack cake form.

PREP TIME: 15 minutes ◆ **BAKE TIME:** 1 hour 20 minutes ◆ **SERVINGS:** 8

Nonstick baking spray
  (with flour)
1 (16-ounce) jar mara-
  schino cherries
1 cup sugar

½ cup vegetable oil
1 cup sour cream
2 large eggs
1 teaspoon vanilla extract
1¾ cups all-purpose flour

2 teaspoons
  baking powder
¼ teaspoon salt
½ cup milk chocolate chips

1. Preheat the oven to 350°F. Mist an 8½-by-4½-inch loaf pan with baking spray and line the pan with a parchment sling (see page 9), with the overhang on the long sides.

2. Reserving the liquid, drain the cherries and pat them dry with a paper towel. Mince enough cherries (in a mini food processor if you have one) to get 1 cup. Measure out ¼ cup of the reserved juice.

3. In a large bowl, using an electric mixer on medium speed, beat the sugar and oil together until combined. Beat in the sour cream, the reserved cherry juice, eggs, and vanilla, just until the eggs are incorporated.

4. In a medium bowl, combine the flour, baking powder, and salt. Add the flour mixture to the sour cream mixture and beat on medium speed, just until the flour is worked into the batter. Fold in the minced cherries and chocolate chips until evenly distributed.

5. Scrape the batter into the prepared loaf pan. Bake for 1 hour 15 minutes to 1 hour 20 minutes, until a toothpick inserted in the center of the cake comes out mostly clean.

6. Transfer the pan to a wire rack to cool completely. Remove the cake from the pan, discard the parchment, and cut into 8 slices to serve.

Blueberry-Lemon Cake

◆ MAKES 1 (8-INCH) SQUARE CAKE ◆

If summertime were a cake, it would taste exactly like this bright berry number: sweet, tart, and incredibly fruity—but without the mess of stained fingers and juice running down your chin!

PREP TIME: 15 minutes ◆ **BAKE TIME:** 40 minutes ◆ **SERVINGS:** 9

Nonstick baking spray (with flour)

12 tablespoons (1½ sticks) unsalted butter, melted

1 cup sugar

2 large eggs

1 tablespoon grated lemon zest

¼ cup fresh lemon juice

1 cup all-purpose flour

1 teaspoon baking powder

⅛ teaspoon salt

½ cup frozen or fresh blueberries

1. Preheat the oven to 350°F. Mist an 8-inch square baking pan with baking spray and line with a parchment sling (see page 9).

2. In a large bowl, using an electric mixer on medium speed, cream the butter and sugar together for 2 to 3 minutes, until light and fluffy. Beat in the eggs, lemon zest, and lemon juice until well combined.

3. In a medium bowl, combine the flour, baking powder, and salt. Add the flour mixture to the lemon mixture and beat on medium speed, just until the flour is worked into the batter. Fold in the blueberries.

4. Scrape the batter into the prepared baking pan. Bake for 35 to 40 minutes, until a toothpick inserted in the center of the cake comes out mostly clean.

5. Transfer the pan to a wire rack to cool completely. Remove the cake from the pan, discard the parchment, and cut the cake into 9 squares to serve.

STORAGE: Will keep tightly covered with plastic wrap or in an airtight container at room temperature for 4 to 5 days.

INGREDIENT TIP: Any frozen blueberries will work in this recipe, but I recommend the smaller wild blueberries. Wild blueberries aren't as juicy as regular blueberries, so they don't turn the cake purple. They are also sweeter than regular blueberries.

Cherry-Almond Cake

◆ MAKES 1 (8-INCH) SQUARE CAKE ◆

Fresh cherries and lots of sliced almonds combine in this delightful take on a classic flavor pairing. A cherry pitter will come in handy for this recipe, but the cherries can also easily be cut in half and pitted.

PREP TIME: 15 minutes ◆ **BAKE TIME:** 35 minutes ◆ **SERVINGS:** 9

Nonstick baking spray (with flour)
8 tablespoons (1 stick) unsalted butter, at room temperature
¾ cup sugar
1 teaspoon vanilla extract

¼ teaspoon almond extract
2 large eggs
1½ cups all-purpose flour
1 teaspoon baking powder
1 teaspoon baking soda

⅛ teaspoon salt
½ cup evaporated milk, whole milk, or buttermilk
¾ cup fresh cherries, stemmed, pitted, and halved
¼ cup sliced almonds

1. Preheat the oven to 350°F. Mist an 8-inch square baking pan with baking spray and line with a parchment sling (see page 9).

2. In a large bowl, using an electric mixer on medium speed, cream the butter and sugar together for 2 to 3 minutes, until light and fluffy. Beat in the vanilla and almond extracts, then add the eggs, one at a time, beating just until each egg is incorporated.

3. In a medium bowl, combine the flour, baking powder, baking soda, and salt. Add the flour mixture to the butter-sugar mixture, a little at a time and alternating with the evaporated milk, mixing well after each addition, until just combined.

4. Scrape the batter into the prepared baking pan. Gently push the cherries into the batter, then sprinkle the almonds on top. Bake for 30 to 35 minutes, until a toothpick inserted in the center of the cake comes out mostly clean.

5. Transfer the pan to a wire rack to cool completely. Remove the cake from the pan, discard the parchment, and cut into 9 squares to serve.

Raspberry White Chocolate Loaf Cake

◆ MAKES 1 (8½-BY-4½-INCH) LOAF CAKE ◆

Another classic pastry flavor combination, white chocolate and raspberry are complementary because they contrast: The sweetness from the white chocolate with the bright flavor of the raspberries scattered throughout this cake make it the perfect balance. This is an elegant treat in a snackable package.

PREP TIME: 10 minutes ◆ **BAKE TIME:** 1 hour 5 minutes ◆ **SERVINGS:** 8

Nonstick baking spray
(with flour)
8 tablespoons (1 stick)
unsalted butter, at room
temperature
1¼ cups sugar
½ cup sour cream

2 large eggs
2 teaspoons vanilla extract
1¾ cups all-purpose flour
1 teaspoon
baking powder
½ teaspoon baking soda
¼ teaspoon salt

¼ cup whole milk
1 cup frozen or fresh
raspberries
½ cup white
chocolate chips

1. Preheat the oven to 350°F. Mist an 8½-by-4½-inch loaf pan with baking spray and line the pan with a parchment sling (see page 9), with the overhang on the long sides.

2. In a large bowl, using an electric mixer on medium speed, cream the butter and sugar together for 2 to 3 minutes, until light and fluffy. Beat in the sour cream, eggs, and vanilla just until incorporated.

3. In a medium bowl, combine the flour, baking powder, baking soda, and salt. Add the flour mixture to the butter-sugar mixture, a little at a time and alternating with the milk, mixing well after each addition, until just combined. Fold in the raspberries and chocolate chips.

4. Scrape the batter into the prepared loaf pan. Bake for 1 hour to 1 hour 5 minutes, until a toothpick inserted in the center of the cake comes out mostly clean.

5. Transfer the pan to a wire rack to cool completely. Remove the cake from the pan, discard the parchment, and cut into 8 slices to serve.

STORAGE: Will keep tightly covered with plastic wrap or in an airtight container at room temperature for 4 to 5 days.

TOP IT OFF: White Chocolate Ganache (page 126) would make the perfect drizzle for this loaf cake.

Orange Loaf Cake

◆ MAKES 1 (8½-BY-4½-INCH) LOAF CAKE ◆

The beloved Creamsicle ice cream bar is turned into a snacking cake loaded with orange juice, orange zest, and orange extract. For an unexpected twist, white chocolate chips are sprinkled in the cake, too.

PREP TIME: 15 minutes ◆ **BAKE TIME:** 1 hour 25 minutes ◆ **SERVINGS:** 8

Nonstick baking spray (with flour)

8 tablespoons (1 stick) unsalted butter, at room temperature

1 cup sugar

½ cup sour cream

2 teaspoons vanilla extract

2 teaspoons orange extract

1 tablespoon grated orange zest

2 large eggs

1¾ cups all-purpose flour

1 teaspoon baking powder

½ teaspoon baking soda

¼ teaspoon salt

¼ cup pulp-free orange juice

Orange gel food coloring (optional)

1 cup white chocolate chips

1. Preheat the oven to 350°F. Mist an 8½-by-4½-inch loaf pan with baking spray and line the pan with a parchment sling (see page 9), with the overhang on the long sides.

2. In a large bowl, using an electric mixer on medium speed, cream the butter and sugar together for 2 to 3 minutes, until light and fluffy. Beat in the sour cream, vanilla, orange extract, orange zest, and eggs, beating just until the eggs are incorporated.

3. In a medium bowl, combine the flour, baking powder, baking soda, and salt. Add the flour mixture to the butter-sugar mixture, a little at a time and alternating with the orange juice (with the food coloring added to it, if using), mixing well after each addition, until just combined. Fold in the white chocolate chips.

4. Scrape the batter into the prepared loaf pan. Bake for 1 hour 20 minutes to 1 hour 25 minutes, until a toothpick inserted in the center of the cake comes out mostly clean.

5. Transfer the pan to a wire rack to cool completely. Remove the cake from the pan, discard the parchment, and cut into 8 slices to serve.

STORAGE: Will keep tightly covered with plastic wrap or in an airtight container at room temperature for 4 to 5 days.

TOP IT OFF: This loaf cake has plenty of orange flavor, but if you want more, drizzle it with White Chocolate Ganache (page 126) with 1 teaspoon grated orange zest stirred in.

Coconut-Lime Cake

◆ MAKES 1 (8-INCH) SQUARE CAKE ◆

Transport yourself to the islands with the classically tropical flavors of coconut and lime. The coconut milk keeps the cake moist and dreamy and while I've included a luscious frosting to top it off, it's also delicious as a poke cake with a glaze instead.

PREP TIME: 15 minutes ◆ **BAKE TIME:** 18 to 20 minutes ◆ **SERVINGS:** 9

FOR THE CAKE
Nonstick baking spray
  (with flour)
8 tablespoons (1 stick)
  unsalted butter, at room
  temperature
¾ cup granulated sugar
3 large egg yolks
½ teaspoon coconut
  flavoring or extract

½ teaspoon vanilla extract
1½ cups all-purpose flour
½ teaspoon
  baking powder
½ teaspoon baking soda
¼ teaspoon salt
¾ cup canned full-fat
  coconut milk
½ cup buttermilk

FOR THE FROSTING
6 ounces cream cheese, at
  room temperature
6 tablespoons (¾ stick)
  unsalted butter, at room
  temperature
1 teaspoon grated
  lime zest
1½ tablespoons fresh
  lime juice
2½ cups powdered sugar

1. **Make the cake:** Preheat the oven to 350°F. Mist an 8-inch square baking pan with baking spray and line with a parchment sling (see page 9).

2. In a large bowl, using an electric mixer on medium speed, cream the butter and granulated sugar together for 2 to 3 minutes, until light and fluffy. Add the egg yolks, coconut flavoring, and vanilla, beating until combined.

3. In a medium bowl, whisk together the flour, baking powder, baking soda, and salt. Set aside.

4. In a small bowl or a large measuring cup, combine the coconut milk and buttermilk.

5. Add the flour mixture to the butter-sugar mixture, a little at a time and alternating with the coconut milk-buttermilk mixture, mixing well after each addition, until just combined.

6. Scrape the batter into the prepared baking pan. Bake for 18 to 20 minutes, until a toothpick inserted in the center of the cake comes out mostly clean.

7. Transfer the pan to a wire rack to cool completely. Remove the cake from the pan, discard the parchment, and place right-side up on a serving plate.

8. **Make the frosting:** In a small bowl, using an electric mixer on medium speed, beat the cream cheese and butter together until smooth. Add the lime zest and lime juice and mix well. Add the powdered sugar and mix until smooth.

9. Once the cake is cooled, top with frosting, then cut into 9 squares to serve.

Cranberry-Ginger Cake

◆ MAKES 1 (8-INCH) SQUARE CAKE ◆

I call for dried cranberries here. The fresh ginger adds a subtle spice, and the combination of cranberries and ginger make this a great little holiday cake.

PREP TIME: 15 minutes ◆ **BAKE TIME:** 35 minutes ◆ **SERVINGS:** 9

Nonstick baking spray
 (with flour)
12 tablespoons (1½ sticks)
 unsalted butter, melted
1 cup sugar

¼ cup whole milk
2 large eggs
1 teaspoon vanilla extract
1 teaspoon finely grated
 peeled fresh ginger

1 cup all-purpose flour
1 teaspoon
 baking powder
⅛ teaspoon salt
½ cup dried cranberries

1. Preheat the oven to 350°F. Mist an 8-inch square baking pan with baking spray and line with a parchment sling (see page 9).

2. In a large bowl, using an electric mixer on medium speed, cream the butter and sugar together for 2 to 3 minutes, until light and fluffy. Beat in the milk, eggs, vanilla, and ginger until the eggs are worked into the batter.

3. In a medium bowl, combine the flour, baking powder, and salt. Add the flour mixture to the butter-sugar mixture and beat on medium speed, just until the flour is worked into the batter. Fold in the cranberries.

4. Scrape the batter into the prepared baking pan. Bake for 30 to 35 minutes, until a toothpick inserted in the center of the cake comes out mostly clean.

5. Transfer the pan to a wire rack to cool completely. Remove the cake from the pan, discard the parchment, and cut into 9 squares to serve.

STORAGE: Will keep tightly covered with plastic wrap or in an airtight container at room temperature for 4 to 5 days.

VARIATION: Substitute dried blueberries, dried cherries—or any other dried fruit that would pair well with ginger—for the cranberries.

Old-Fashioned Lemon Cake

When life gives you lemons, and even when it doesn't, this tried-and-true, tender cake is sure to brighten up any day. It is my go-to cheer-up-a-friend cake because it pairs well with brightly colored napkins for a sweet delivery of sunshine.

PREP TIME: 15 minutes ◆ **BAKE TIME:** 30 to 35 minutes ◆ **SERVINGS:** 9

Nonstick baking spray (with flour)
8 tablespoons (1 stick) unsalted butter, at room temperature
1 cup sugar

2 large eggs
1½ cups all-purpose flour
½ teaspoon baking powder
½ teaspoon baking soda
¼ teaspoon salt

½ cup buttermilk
2 teaspoons grated lemon zest
2 tablespoons fresh lemon juice

1. Preheat the oven to 350°F. Mist an 8-inch square baking pan with baking spray and line with a parchment sling (see page 9).

2. In a large bowl, with an electric mixer on medium speed, cream the butter and sugar together for 2 to 3 minutes, until light and fluffy. Add the eggs, one at a time, beating just until each egg is incorporated.

3. In a medium bowl, whisk together the flour, baking powder, baking soda, and salt. Set aside.

4. In a glass measuring cup, combine the buttermilk, lemon zest, and lemon juice.

5. Add the flour mixture to the butter-sugar mixture, a little at a time and alternating with the buttermilk-lemon mixture, mixing well after each addition, until just combined.

6. Scrape the batter into the prepared pan. Bake for 30 to 35 minutes, until a toothpick inserted in the center of the cake comes out mostly clean.

7. Transfer the cake to a wire rack to cool for 10 minutes in the pan. Remove from the pan and set on the wire rack to cool completely. Discard the parchment and cut the cake into 9 squares to serve.

Peach Cobbler Coffee Cake

◆ MAKES 1 (8½-BY-4½-INCH) LOAF CAKE ◆

Sweet peaches, a walnut crumb topping, and an irresistibly rich and moist cake make this recipe one that is sure to become a go-to family favorite. Drizzle a bit of Cinnamon Glaze (page 129) over the top if you want to truly knock socks off.

PREP TIME: 15 minutes ◆ **BAKE TIME:** 50 to 55 minutes ◆ **SERVINGS:** 8

FOR THE CRUMB TOPPING

½ cup chopped walnuts

½ cup all-purpose flour

¼ cup packed light brown sugar

½ teaspoon ground cinnamon

⅛ teaspoon ground nutmeg

4 tablespoons (½ stick) unsalted butter, at room temperature

FOR THE CAKE

¾ cup granulated sugar

¼ cup sour cream

¼ cup buttermilk

2 large eggs

1 teaspoon vanilla extract

2 cups all-purpose flour

1 teaspoon ground cinnamon

½ teaspoon baking powder

½ teaspoon baking soda

1 teaspoon salt

2 cups sliced fresh peaches

1. Preheat the oven to 325°F. Mist an 8½-by-4½-inch loaf pan with baking spray and line the pan with a parchment sling (see page 9), with the overhang on the long sides.

2. **Make the crumb topping:** In a medium bowl, stir together the walnuts, flour, brown sugar, cinnamon, and nutmeg. Using a pastry cutter, a fork, or two knives, cut in the butter until the mixture is crumbly and resembles wet sand. Set aside.

3. **Make the cake:** In a large bowl, using an electric mixer on medium speed, whisk the granulated sugar, sour cream, and buttermilk together until combined. Beat in the eggs and vanilla until well combined.

4. In a medium bowl, whisk together the flour, cinnamon, baking powder, baking soda, and salt. Add the flour mixture, a little at a time, to the sour cream mixture, beating until just combined. Fold in the peaches.

5. Scrape the batter into the prepared pan. Sprinkle the crumb topping on the batter, evenly distributing it. Bake for 50 to 55 minutes, until a toothpick inserted in the center of the cake comes out mostly clean and the top is golden brown.

6. Transfer the pan to a wire rack to cool completely. Remove the cake from the pan, discard the parchment, and cut into 8 slices to serve.

INGREDIENT TIP: Frozen or canned peaches can be used in lieu of fresh peaches. When using frozen, thaw and drain the peaches first. For canned, drain off the liquid.

Strawberry Milkshake Cake

◆ MAKES 1 (8-INCH) SQUARE CAKE ◆

Want all the flavors of a strawberry milkshake but without having to get out the blender? Look no further than this crowd-pleasing cake for all ages. I intensify the pink color of the cake with food coloring, but it's completely optional.

PREP TIME: 15 minutes ◆ **BAKE TIME:** 30 to 35 minutes ◆ **SERVINGS:** 9

Nonstick baking spray (with flour)
5 tablespoons unsalted butter, at room temperature
1 cup sugar
2 large eggs

1½ cups all-purpose flour
1 tablespoon baking powder
½ teaspoon salt
¾ cup whole milk
⅓ cup strawberry milk powder (such as Nestlé)

Dark pink food coloring (optional)
Homemade Whipped Cream (page 130)
Sliced fresh strawberries, for garnish (optional)

1. Preheat the oven to 350°F. Mist an 8-inch square baking pan with baking spray and line with a parchment sling (see page 9).

2. In a large bowl, with an electric mixer on medium speed, cream together the butter and sugar for 2 to 3 minutes, until light and fluffy. Add the eggs, one at a time, beating just until each egg is incorporated.

3. In a medium bowl, whisk together the flour, baking powder, and salt. Add the flour mixture to the butter-sugar mixture, a little at a time, and beat until just combined.

4. In a measuring cup, stir to combine the milk and strawberry powder. Slowly add it to the batter, mixing until just combined. If desired, add a few drops of dark pink gel food coloring.

5. Scrape the batter into the prepared pan. Bake for 30 to 35 minutes, until a toothpick inserted in the center of the cake comes out mostly clean.

6. Transfer the pan to a wire rack to cool completely. Remove the cake from the pan, discard the parchment, and cut into 9 squares to serve. Garnish each square with whipped cream and strawberries (if using).

Blueberry Skillet Cake

✦ MAKES 1 (8-INCH) ROUND CAKE ✦

We frequent a local U-pick blueberry farm nearly every year, so I have an abundance of quick and easy blueberry recipes that make the most of the season, but this recipe is so versatile you could use just about any fruit you'd like.

PREP TIME: 15 minutes ✦ **BAKE TIME:** 30 minutes ✦ **SERVINGS:** 8

8 tablespoons (1 stick) unsalted butter, at room temperature

½ cup sugar

1 large egg

2 tablespoons almond milk

1 teaspoon vanilla extract

1 cup all-purpose flour

2 cups fresh blueberries, divided

¼ cup sliced almonds

1. Preheat the oven to 350°F

2. In a large bowl, using an electric mixer on medium speed, cream the butter and sugar together for 2 to 3 minutes, until light and fluffy. Beat in the egg, almond milk, and vanilla until well combined.

3. Gradually add the flour, a little at a time, beating until just combined. Fold in 1½ cups of blueberries.

4. Scrape the batter into an 8-inch cast-iron skillet. Arrange the remaining ½ cup of blueberries and sliced almonds on top of the cake. Bake for about 30 minutes, or until a toothpick inserted in the center of the cake comes out mostly clean.

5. Cool for 15 minutes on a wire rack, then cut into 8 wedges and serve directly from the skillet.

SUBSTITUTION: Whole milk can be used in place of almond milk.

VARIATION: Halve the amount of blueberries and replace with sliced strawberries and you have yourself a patriotic cake in a flash.

INGREDIENT TIP: Frozen blueberries will work in this recipe, but I recommend the smaller wild blueberries. Wild blueberries aren't as juicy as regular blueberries, so they don't turn the cake purple.

Bananas Foster Loaf Cake

◆ MAKES 1 (8½-BY-4½-INCH) LOAF CAKE ◆

Bananas Foster is a delicious dessert from the famous Brennan's restaurant in New Orleans, where bananas and a buttery rum sauce are flambéed tableside and served with ice cream. This easy-to-make, moist and tender cake brings all the flavors of that famed dessert but requires zero travel and no blow torch. *Laissez les bons temps rouler!*

PREP TIME: 15 minutes ◆ **BAKE TIME:** 1 hour 10 minutes ◆ **SERVINGS:** 8

FOR THE CAKE
Nonstick baking spray (with flour)
⅓ cup coconut oil
5 large egg yolks
1 teaspoon vanilla extract
1 teaspoon rum extract
1¾ cups all-purpose flour
1 cup granulated sugar

2 teaspoons baking powder
1 teaspoon salt
¾ cup whole milk

FOR THE TOPPING
2 tablespoons unsalted butter, at room temperature

¼ cup packed light brown sugar
1 teaspoon vanilla extract
1 teaspoon rum extract
¼ teaspoon ground cinnamon
2 bananas, sliced

1. **Make the cake:** Preheat the oven to 350°F. Mist an 8½-by-4½-inch loaf pan with baking spray and line the pan with a parchment sling (see page 9), with the overhang on the long sides.

2. In a large bowl, with an electric mixer on medium speed, beat the coconut oil, egg yolks, vanilla, and rum extract.

3. In a medium bowl, whisk together the flour, granulated sugar, baking powder, and salt. Add the flour mixture to the oil-egg mixture, a little at a time and alternating with the milk, mixing well after each addition, until just combined.

4. Scrape the batter into the prepared loaf pan. Bake for 1 hour to 1 hour 10 minutes, until a toothpick inserted in the center of the cake comes out mostly clean.

5. Transfer the pan to a wire rack to cool completely. Remove the cake from the pan, discard the parchment, and set the cake right-side up on a serving plate.

6. **Meanwhile, make the topping:** In a small saucepan, melt the butter over medium heat. Add the brown sugar, vanilla, rum extract, and cinnamon and mix well. Continue to cook until the sugar is completely dissolved, then add the banana slices. Toss to coat. Remove from the heat and allow to cool slightly before serving.

7. When ready to serve, slice the loaf cake into 8 slices and top each slice with the topping. Serve immediately.

Chocolate Strawberry Ice Cream Cake ◆ Page 66

Make Mine Chocolate

Hot Cocoa Cake

◆ MAKES 1 (8-INCH) SQUARE CAKE ◆

Just as the name suggests, this cake is reminiscent of taking a sip of hot cocoa. It's chocolaty, with marshmallows throughout. The cake works best using the diminutive mallow "bits" in the batter, but if you love marshmallows, as I do, be sure to include some extra on top—either additional bits, or the slightly larger mini marshmallows.

PREP TIME: 15 minutes ◆ **BAKE TIME:** 35 minutes ◆ **SERVINGS:** 9

Nonstick baking spray (with flour)

8 tablespoons (1 stick) unsalted butter, at room temperature

¾ cup sugar

1 teaspoon vanilla extract

2 large eggs

1 cup all-purpose flour

¼ cup unsweetened Dutch process cocoa powder

1 teaspoon baking powder

1 teaspoon baking soda

2 tablespoons hot water

3 ounces hot cocoa mix (about 4 packets), without marshmallows

½ cup marshmallow bits

1. Preheat the oven to 350°F. Mist an 8-inch square baking pan with baking spray and line with a parchment sling (see page 9).

2. In a large bowl, using an electric mixer on medium speed, cream the butter and sugar together for 2 to 3 minutes, until light and fluffy. Beat in the vanilla, then add the eggs, one at a time, beating just until each egg is incorporated.

3. In a medium bowl, combine the flour, cocoa powder, baking powder, and baking soda. Set aside.

4. In a mug, microwave the hot water for 30 seconds. Pour the hot cocoa mix into the mug and stir until dissolved.

5. Add the flour mixture to the butter-sugar mixture, a little at a time and alternating with the hot cocoa mixture, beating well after each addition, until just combined. Fold in the marshmallow bits.

6. Scrape the batter into the prepared baking pan. Bake for 30 to 35 minutes, until a toothpick inserted in the center of the cake comes out mostly clean.

7. Transfer the pan to a wire rack to cool completely. Remove the cake from the pan, discard the parchment paper, and cut into 9 squares to serve.

STORAGE: Will keep tightly covered with plastic wrap or in an airtight container at room temperature for 4 to 5 days.

TOP IT OFF: As a fun addition, top the cake with a layer of mini marshmallows about 5 minutes before the cake is done baking and let them brown up. Sprinkle a very light dusting of hot cocoa mix on top of the marshmallows.

Marbled Loaf Cake

◆ MAKES 1 (8½-BY-4½-INCH) LOAF CAKE ◆

A marbled cake with both vanilla and chocolate solves the conundrum of which flavor you're in the mood for, making it easy to have both. It's great with coffee but even better as a vehicle for a scoop of ice cream.

PREP TIME: 15 minutes ◆ **BAKE TIME:** 1 hour 5 minutes ◆ **SERVINGS:** 8

Nonstick baking spray (with flour)
8 tablespoons (1 stick) unsalted butter, at room temperature
1¼ cups sugar

½ cup sour cream
2 large eggs
2 teaspoons vanilla extract
1¾ cups all-purpose flour
1 teaspoon baking powder

½ teaspoon baking soda
¼ teaspoon salt
¼ cup whole milk
2 tablespoons unsweetened Dutch process cocoa powder

1. Preheat the oven to 350°F. Mist an 8½-by-4½-inch loaf pan with baking spray and line the pan with a parchment sling (see page 9), with the overhang on the long sides.

2. In a large bowl, using an electric mixer on medium speed, cream the butter and sugar together for 2 to 3 minutes, until light and fluffy. Beat in the sour cream, eggs, and vanilla until the eggs are just incorporated.

3. In a medium bowl, combine the flour, baking powder, baking soda, and salt. Add the flour mixture to the butter-sugar mixture, a little at a time and alternating with the milk, beating well after each addition, until just combined.

4. Transfer about 1 cup of the batter to a small bowl. Stir in the cocoa until completely combined.

5. Pour half the vanilla batter into the prepared loaf pan. Pour half the chocolate batter on top of the vanilla batter. Repeat with the remaining halves of the vanilla and chocolate batters. With a butter knife or skewer, swirl the batters together, taking care not to mix them too much. Bake for 1 hour to 1 hour 5 minutes, until a toothpick inserted in the center of the cake comes out mostly clean.

6. Transfer the pan to a wire rack to cool completely. Remove the cake from the pan, discard the parchment, and cut into 8 slices to serve.

STORAGE: Will keep tightly covered with plastic wrap or in an airtight container at room temperature for 4 to 5 days.

TOP IT OFF: Depending on whether you are a vanilla or chocolate fan, you can drizzle it with Chocolate Ganache (page 126), Vanilla Glaze (page 129), or both!

Chocolate Strawberry Ice Cream Cake

◆ MAKES 1 (8-INCH) SQUARE CAKE ◆

Ice cream and cake make a great pair, but ice cream set on top of cake makes life much sweeter. This tasty combo pairs a rich chocolate base with a homemade strawberry custard that is spread and then frozen on top of the baked cake—instant ice cream cake! It adds a bit of extra time for the cake to freeze, but it rivals anything you can buy in the store.

PREP TIME: 20 minutes, plus 4 hours to freeze ◆ **BAKE TIME:** 25 minutes
SERVINGS: 9

FOR THE CAKE
Nonstick baking spray
   (with flour)
⅓ cup boiling water
⅓ cup sour cream
¼ cup vegetable oil
¼ cup unsweetened Dutch
   process cocoa powder
1 teaspoon vanilla extract
1 large egg

¾ cup sugar
½ cup all-purpose flour
½ teaspoon
   baking powder
½ teaspoon baking soda
¼ teaspoon salt

FOR THE
STRAWBERRY CREAM

1 cup heavy
   (whipping) cream

¾ cup plus 2 tablespoons
   sweetened
   condensed milk
½ cup finely chopped
   hulled strawberries (5 to
   7 strawberries)
1 teaspoon vanilla extract

1. **Make the cake:** Preheat the oven to 350°F. Mist an 8-inch square baking pan with baking spray and line with a parchment sling (see page 9).

2. In a medium bowl, whisk the boiling water, sour cream, oil, cocoa, and vanilla together until the cocoa and sour cream are fully combined. It will be thick and creamy. Whisk in the egg.

3. In a large bowl, combine the sugar, flour, baking powder, baking soda, and salt. Add the cocoa mixture and whisk until smooth.

4. Scrape the batter into the prepared baking pan. Bake for 20 to 25 minutes, until a toothpick inserted in the center of the cake comes out mostly clean.

5. Transfer the pan to a wire rack to cool completely.

6. **Meanwhile, make the strawberry cream:** In a large bowl, using an electric mixer on medium speed, beat the cream until soft peaks form. Increase the mixer speed to high and beat until firm peaks form. (When you pull your beater out of the whipped cream and turn it upside down, it should form a peak and hold its shape without falling over.) Fold in the condensed milk, strawberries, and vanilla until incorporated.

7. Pour the strawberry cream on top of the cooled cake and place in the freezer for 3 to 4 hours until the cream is firm.

8. Cut the cake into 9 squares to serve.

....

STORAGE: Will keep tightly covered with plastic wrap or in an airtight container in the freezer for 4 to 5 days.

....

VARIATION: Substitute finely chopped maraschino cherries, fresh blackberries, or fresh raspberries for the strawberries.

Zucchini Chocolate Chip Loaf Cake

◆ MAKES 1 (8½-BY-4½-INCH) LOAF CAKE ◆

I was a little bit late to the zucchini-in-desserts party due to my irrational fear of vegetables. However zucchini adds a wonderful texture and moistness to baked goods. Its taste is so mild that there's no reason to tell anyone—and I'm betting you'll forget you even added it in there, too.

PREP TIME: 15 minutes ◆ **BAKE TIME:** 1 hour 20 minutes ◆ **SERVINGS:** 8

Nonstick baking spray
 (with flour)
½ cup vegetable oil
¾ cup granulated sugar
⅓ cup packed light
 brown sugar

3 large eggs
2 teaspoons vanilla extract
2 cups shredded zucchini
 (about 2 medium
 zucchini)
2 cups all-purpose flour

½ teaspoon
 baking powder
½ teaspoon baking soda
¼ teaspoon salt
¼ cup milk chocolate chips

1. Preheat the oven to 350°F. Mist an 8½-by-4½-inch loaf pan with baking spray and line the pan with a parchment sling (see page 9), with the overhang on the long sides.

2. In a large bowl, using an electric mixer on medium speed, beat the oil, granulated and brown sugars, eggs, and vanilla together until well combined. Add the zucchini and beat until fully incorporated.

3. In a medium bowl, combine the flour, baking powder, baking soda, and salt. Add the flour mixture to the zucchini mixture and whisk until the batter is smooth. Fold in the chocolate chips.

4. Scrape the batter into the prepared loaf pan. Bake for 1 hour 20 minutes, or until a toothpick inserted in the center of the cake comes out mostly clean.

5. Transfer the pan to a wire rack to cool completely. Remove the cake from the pan, discard the parchment, and cut into 8 slices to serve.

TOP IT OFF: Drizzle with Chocolate Ganache (page 126) before slicing.

Minty Chocolate Cake

◆ MAKES 1 (8-INCH) SQUARE CAKE ◆

The flavor combination of indulgent chocolate and refreshing mint is something truly heaven-sent in my opinion. It is among my favorite combinations—just ask my neighborhood Girl Scout. If you're a fan of Thin Mints, Andes Mints, or Junior Mints (and you know who you are), this is this cake for you.

PREP TIME: 20 minutes ◆ **BAKE TIME:** 25 minutes ◆ **SERVINGS:** 9

Nonstick baking spray
(with flour)
1½ cups all-purpose flour
1 cup sugar
6 tablespoons unsweet-
ened Dutch process
cocoa powder
½ teaspoon baking soda

½ teaspoon
baking powder
½ teaspoon salt
¾ cup whole milk
¼ cup vegetable oil, plus
1 tablespoon
2 large eggs

1 teaspoon pepper-
mint extract
½ cup semisweet choco-
late chips
1 cup Andes crème de
menthe mints
1 tablespoon vegetable oil

1. Preheat the oven to 350°F. Mist an 8-inch square baking pan with baking spray and line with a parchment sling (see page 9).

2. In a large bowl, whisk together the flour, sugar, cocoa, baking soda, and baking powder. Add the milk, ¼ cup of oil, the eggs, and peppermint extract, whisking until combined. Fold in the chocolate chips.

3. Scrape the batter into the prepared baking pan.

4. In a microwave-safe bowl, melt the Andes mints with the remaining 1 tablespoon of vegetable oil a few seconds at a time, mixing until smooth. Place the melted chocolate in a piping bag (or a zip-top bag with a corner cut out) and pipe horizontal lines across the batter. Use a knife to gently pull it through the lines of melted chocolate to create a design.

5. Bake for 25 to 30 minutes, until a toothpick inserted in the center of the cake comes out mostly clean.

6. Transfer the cake to a wire rack to cool for 10 minutes in the pan. Remove from the pan and set on the wire rack to cool completely. Discard the parchment and cut the cake into 9 squares to serve.

Chocolate Eggnog Cake

◆ MAKES 1 (8-INCH) SQUARE CAKE ◆

Just when you thought eggnog was reserved for drinking, this cake comes along and shakes things up. This small but mighty cake comes together lightning fast, making it perfect during the holiday season when guests often drop by on short notice.

PREP TIME: 20 minutes ◆ **BAKE TIME:** 20 to 25 minutes ◆ **SERVINGS:** 9

Nonstick baking spray (with flour)

4 tablespoons (½ stick) unsalted butter, at room temperature

2 ounces unsweetened chocolate

1 cup all-purpose flour

1 cup sugar

2 teaspoons baking powder

½ teaspoon ground cinnamon

½ teaspoon ground nutmeg

1 cup eggnog

1 teaspoon vanilla extract

1. Preheat the oven to 350°F. Mist an 8-inch square baking pan with baking spray and line with a parchment sling (see page 9).

2. In a microwave-safe bowl, melt the butter and chocolate, stirring to combine.

3. In a medium bowl, whisk together the flour, sugar, baking powder, cinnamon, and nutmeg. Stir in the eggnog and vanilla. Fold in the melted chocolate.

4. Scrape the batter into the prepared pan. Bake for 20 to 25 minutes, until a tooth-pick inserted in the center of the cake comes out mostly clean.

5. Transfer the cake to a wire rack to cool for 10 minutes in the pan. Remove from the pan and set on the wire rack to cool completely. Discard the parchment and cut the cake into 9 squares to serve.

TOP IT OFF: Make Homemade Whipped Cream (page 130), replacing the vanilla extract with eggnog and adding an additional 2 tablespoons of sugar. Top each cake square with a dollop of the whipped cream to further enhances the subtle eggnog flavor in this cake. But, if there's no time for whipping cream and your guests are arriving at any minute, once the squares are cut, place a small holiday cookie cutter on top of the square to serve as a pattern, and dust the cake top inside the cutter with powdered sugar. When you remove the cookie cutter, you'll have a fun holiday design left behind.

Chocolate Coconut Cake

The marriage of chocolate and coconut is one that is sure to stand the test of time. And speaking of marriages, I once attended a wedding where the groom loved Almond Joys so much that they served coconut brownies adorned with the candy instead of a groom's cake. This cake is reminiscent of those chocolate-coconut bites of wonder.

PREP TIME: 20 minutes ◆ **BAKE TIME:** 30 to 35 minutes ◆ **SERVINGS:** 9

Nonstick baking spray (with flour)

1 cup boiling water

1 cup canned coconut cream, at room temperature

⅓ cup coconut oil, melted

½ cup unsweetened Dutch process cocoa powder

½ teaspoon vanilla extract

2 large eggs

1½ cups all-purpose flour

¾ cup unsweetened shredded coconut

1 cup sugar

1 teaspoon baking powder

½ teaspoon salt

1. Preheat the oven to 350°F. Mist an 8-inch square baking pan with baking spray and line with a parchment sling (see page 9).

2. In a large bowl, whisk the boiling water, coconut cream, coconut oil, cocoa, and vanilla together until the cocoa is fully combined. It will be thick and creamy. Whisk in the eggs, one at a time, mixing well after each addition.

3. In a medium bowl, combine the flour, shredded coconut, sugar, baking powder, and salt. Add the flour mixture to the cocoa-egg mixture and whisk until smooth.

4. Scrape the batter into the prepared baking pan. Bake for 30 to 35 minutes, until a toothpick inserted in the center of the cake comes out mostly clean.

5. Transfer the cake to a wire rack to cool for 10 minutes in the pan. Remove from the pan and set on the wire rack to cool completely. Discard the parchment and cut the cake into 9 squares to serve.

TOP IT OFF: Chocolate Ganache (page 126) sprinkled with some coconut flakes will send this cake over the top and make for a beautiful presentation.

Cocoa Crunch Cake

You'll be hard-pressed to declare what's better about this cake: the cake or the crunch topping made with chocolate-coated breakfast cereal. One bite of this delicious combination will leave you wanting to add it to every cake from now to eternity. I like layering a bit of whipped cream in between the two layers of choco-late to give it something to hang on to.

PREP TIME: 20 minutes ◆ **BAKE TIME:** 30 to 35 minutes ◆ **SERVINGS:** 9

FOR THE CAKE
Nonstick baking spray
   (with flour)
1 cup all-purpose flour
1 cup granulated sugar
¼ cup unsweetened Dutch
   process cocoa powder
½ teaspoon
   baking powder
½ teaspoon baking soda

¼ teaspoon salt
½ cup vegetable oil
½ cup buttermilk
1 large egg
½ cup hot water
½ cup mini choco-
   late chips

**FOR THE
COCOA CRUNCH**
½ cup chocolate chips

2 teaspoons vegetable oil
1 cup chocolate cereal
   (such as Cocoa Pebbles)

**FOR THE
WHIPPED TOPPING**
1 cup heavy
   (whipping) cream
2 tablespoons
   powdered sugar
½ teaspoon vanilla extract

1. **Make the cake:** Preheat the oven to 350°F. Mist an 8-inch square baking pan with baking spray and line with a parchment sling (see page 9).

2. In a medium bowl, whisk together the flour, granulated sugar, cocoa, baking powder, baking soda, and salt. Add the oil, buttermilk, and egg, beating to com-bine. Add the hot water and continue mixing until the batter is smooth. Fold in the chocolate chips.

3. Scrape the batter into the prepared baking pan. Bake for 30 to 35 minutes, until a toothpick inserted in the center of the cake comes out mostly clean.

4. Transfer the pan to a wire rack to cool completely.

5. **Meanwhile, make the cocoa crunch:** Line a baking sheet with parchment paper. In a microwave-safe bowl, in 30-second intervals, melt the chocolate chips with the vegetable oil. Once melted and smooth, add the chocolate cereal to the melted chocolate, gently stirring until completely coated. Evenly spread onto the pre-pared baking sheet and place in the freezer for about 10 minutes.

6. **Make the whipped topping:** While you wait for the crunch coating to harden, in a large bowl, using an electric mixer on medium speed, beat the cream, powdered sugar, and vanilla together until stiff peaks form.

7. Remove the cooled cake from the pan, discard the parchment, and set the cake right-side up on a serving plate. Top the cake with the whipped topping and sprinkle with the crunch. Cut the cake into 9 squares to serve.

Lagniappe Cake

◆ MAKES 1 (8-INCH) SQUARE CAKE ◆

Lagniappe in Cajun-French means "something extra." And like clockwork, after every Easter or Halloween I find myself with extra chocolate candy hanging around. A couple of years ago I decided to create small-batch cakes with the leftovers, calling them Lagniappe Cakes. Sometimes they might have Snickers and other times Kit Kats, but there's always something a little extra about these snack-size cakes.

PREP TIME: 20 minutes ◆ **BAKE TIME:** 30 to 35 minutes ◆ **SERVINGS:** 9

Nonstick baking spray (with flour)
1½ cups all-purpose flour
¼ teaspoon baking soda
⅛ teaspoon salt

8 tablespoons (1 stick) unsalted butter, at room temperature
1 cup sugar
2 large eggs
1 teaspoon vanilla extract

½ cup buttermilk
1 cup chopped mini peanut butter cups or mini candy bar of your choice

1. Preheat the oven to 350°F. Mist an 8-inch square baking pan with baking spray and line with a parchment sling (see page 9).

2. In a medium bowl, whisk together the flour, baking soda, and salt. Set aside.

3. In a large bowl, using an electric mixer on medium speed, cream together the butter and sugar for 2 to 3 minutes, or until fluffy. Add the eggs, one at a time, beating just until each egg is incorporated. Beat in the vanilla.

4. Add the flour mixture to the butter-sugar mixture, a little at a time and alternating with the buttermilk, mixing well after each addition, until just combined. Stir in the peanut butter cups.

5. Scrape the batter into the prepared baking pan. Bake for 30 to 35 minutes, until a toothpick inserted in the center of the cake comes out mostly clean.

6. Transfer the pan to a wire rack to cool completely. Remove the cake from the pan, discard the parchment, and cut into 9 squares to serve.

TOP IT OFF: If you just can't get enough peanut butter flavor, try drizzling this with Peanut Butter Glaze (page 128). Or for a more faithful imitation of an actual peanut butter cup, try it topped with Chocolate Ganache (page 126).

VARIATION: Use this recipe as a simple base and substitute whatever chocolate candy you have on hand. Whoppers may not appeal to trick-or-treaters (why do those get left behind?), but they are delicious as a cake topper.

Spicy Mexi-Chocolate Cake

In the winter months, I love curling up with a cup of spicy Mexican hot chocolate. But for all those times when I crave those cozy flavors without the heat, I turn to my favorite drink in cake form. If you have a specialty retailer carrying Mexican chocolate or vanilla, then certainly use that for a more authentic offering.

PREP TIME: 20 minutes ◆ **BAKE TIME:** 30 to 35 minutes ◆ **SERVINGS:** 9

Nonstick baking spray (with flour)

8 tablespoons (1 stick) unsalted butter, at room temperature

6 ounces bittersweet chocolate (or 2 discs Mexican chocolate, such as Ibarra), coarsely chopped

2 tablespoons brewed espresso coffee

1 cup water

1½ cups all-purpose flour

1 cup sugar

1 teaspoon ground cinnamon

1 teaspoon baking soda

½ teaspoon cayenne pepper

¼ teaspoon salt

2 large eggs

1 teaspoon vanilla extract (Mexican if you can find it)

½ teaspoon almond extract

1. Preheat the oven to 350°F. Mist an 8-inch square baking pan with baking spray and line with a parchment sling (see page 9).

2. In a large saucepan, melt the butter over medium heat. Whisk in the chocolate and espresso, followed by the water, continuing to whisk until smooth. Remove from the heat and set aside to cool.

3. In a large bowl, using an electric mixer on medium speed, whisk together the flour, sugar, cinnamon, baking soda, cayenne, and salt. Beat in the eggs, vanilla, and almond extract.

4. Once the butter-chocolate mixture is cool to the touch, slowly pour it into the flour-egg mixture, beating to combine.

5. Scrape the batter into the prepared baking pan. Bake for 30 to 35 minutes, until a toothpick inserted in the center of the cake comes out mostly clean.

6. Transfer the pan to a wire rack to cool completely. Remove the cake from the pan, discard the parchment, and cut into 9 squares to serve.

TOP IT OFF: A light dusting of powdered sugar is all this cake needs, but Homemade Whipped Cream (page 130) mixed with 1 teaspoon of ground cinnamon gives it a bit more sizzle.

INGREDIENT TIP: If you're able to locate Ibarra chocolate at a specialty grocery store, you'll need less than the bittersweet chocolate due to its intense chocolate taste.

Dalmatian Brownie Cake

Called the "Dalmatian" because its white chocolate chips resemble the spots on a Dalmatian (though the reverse of the dog's black spots), this cake can be enjoyed straight from the oven. No fuss, no frills, a brownie cake in less than 30 minutes.

PREP TIME: 20 minutes ◆ **BAKE TIME:** 25 minutes ◆ **SERVINGS:** 9

Nonstick baking spray (with flour)
¾ cup semisweet chocolate chips

8 tablespoons (1 stick) unsalted butter, at room temperature
2 large eggs
1 cup sugar

1 teaspoon vanilla extract
1 cup all-purpose flour
1 cup white chocolate chips, divided

1. Preheat the oven to 350°F. Mist an 8-inch square baking pan with baking spray and line with a parchment sling (see page 9).

2. In a double boiler (or a heatproof medium bowl set over a pan of simmering water), melt the semisweet chocolate chips and butter, stirring until melted. Set aside to cool.

3. In a medium bowl, using an electric mixer on medium speed, beat the eggs, sugar, and vanilla. Fold in the cooled chocolate mixture and then the flour, mixing until well combined. Fold in ½ cup of white chocolate chips.

4. Scrape the batter into the prepared baking pan. Sprinkle the batter with the remaining ½ cup of white chocolate chips. Bake for 25 minutes, or until a toothpick inserted in the center of the cake comes out mostly clean.

5. Transfer the pan to a wire rack to cool completely. Remove the cake from the pan, discard the parchment, and cut into 9 squares to serve.

Southern Chocolate Mayo Cake

◆ MAKES 1 (8-INCH) SQUARE CAKE ◆

This clever recipe for chocolate cake substitutes mayonnaise for eggs, oil, and butter—a popular hack during the Great Depression when baking supplies were rationed. And if you're wondering what makes it "Southern," well, that's because you won't find a Southerner around who doesn't have a favorite mayonnaise brand nor one who will tell you it's ever okay to substitute salad dressing for mayonnaise in this recipe.

PREP TIME: 20 minutes ◆ **BAKE TIME:** 25 to 30 minutes ◆ **SERVINGS:** 9

Nonstick baking spray (with flour)
2 cups all-purpose flour
1 cup sugar

6 tablespoons unsweetened Dutch process cocoa powder
2 teaspoons baking soda
1 cup mayonnaise

¾ cup whole milk
¾ cup warm water
1 teaspoon vanilla extract
½ cup mini chocolate chips

1. Preheat the oven to 350°F. Mist an 8-inch square baking pan with baking spray and line with a parchment sling (see page 9).

2. In a medium bowl, whisk together the flour, sugar, cocoa, and baking soda. Add the mayonnaise, milk, water, and vanilla and mix until evenly combined.

3. Scrape the batter into the prepared baking pan. Sprinkle the mini chocolate chips on top of the cake. Bake for 25 to 30 minutes, until a toothpick inserted in the center of the cake comes out mostly clean.

4. Transfer the pan to a wire rack to cool completely. Remove the cake from the pan, discard the parchment, and cut into 9 squares to serve.

....

TOP IT OFF: I add the mini chocolate chips when I know I'm not going to be topping the cake. But for special occasions I'll leave the chips out and instead top the cake with a simple Homemade Whipped Cream (page 130) or add double chocolaty goodness with Small-Batch Chocolate Buttercream (page 133).

German Chocolate Cake

◆ MAKES 1 (8-INCH) SQUARE CAKE ◆

What's better than German chocolate cake? A smaller portion! Say goodbye to boxed mixes and unmanageable quantities and hello to the same classic chocolate cake you know and love, complete with a decadently rich homemade caramel-coconut-pecan topping.

PREP TIME: 20 minutes ◆ **BAKE TIME:** 30 minutes ◆ **SERVINGS:** 9

FOR THE CAKE
Nonstick baking spray
  (with flour)
4 ounces sweet baking
  chocolate
½ cup (1 stick) unsalted
  butter, at room
  temperature
1 cup granulated sugar

2 large eggs
1 teaspoon vanilla extract
1½ cups all-purpose flour
1 teaspoon
  baking powder
½ teaspoon baking soda
½ teaspoon salt
½ cup buttermilk

FOR THE FROSTING
½ cup evaporated milk
½ cup packed light
  brown sugar
2 large egg yolks,
  lightly beaten
4 tablespoons (½ stick)
  unsalted butter
½ teaspoon vanilla extract
1 cup sweetened
  shredded coconut
½ cup chopped pecans

1. **Make the cake:** Preheat the oven to 350°F. Mist an 8-inch square baking pan with baking spray and line with a parchment sling (see page 9).

2. In a double boiler (or a heatproof bowl over a saucepan of simmering water), melt the chocolate, stirring to combine. Remove from the heat and allow to cool.

3. In a large bowl, using an electric mixer on medium speed, cream the butter and granulated sugar together for 2 to 3 minutes, until light and fluffy. Add the eggs, one at a time, and mix until thoroughly combined. Stir in the vanilla and cooled melted chocolate.

4. In a medium bowl, whisk together the flour, baking powder, baking soda, and salt. Add the flour mixture to the butter-sugar mixture, a little at a time and alternating with the buttermilk, mixing well after each addition, until just combined.

5. Scrape the batter into the prepared baking pan. Bake for 30 minutes, or until a toothpick inserted in the center of the cake comes out mostly clean.

6. Transfer the cake to a wire rack to cool for 10 minutes in the pan. Remove from the pan and set on the wire rack to cool completely. Discard the parchment.

7. **Make the frosting:** In a medium saucepan, combine the evaporated milk, brown sugar, egg yolks, butter, and vanilla. Cook over medium heat, stirring occasionally, until thickened. Remove from the heat. Stir in the coconut and pecans. Let cool until thick enough to spread.

8. Spread the cake with the frosting, then cut into 9 squares to serve.

TIP: Due to its gooey frosting, if you're planning on taking this cake somewhere, it's best transported in its pan uncut. After the cake has cooled and you've removed the parchment, carefully return the cake to the pan before frosting. Cut and serve once you reach your destination.

Chocolate Sin Cake

◆ MAKES 1 (8-INCH) SQUARE CAKE ◆

Ultimate chocolate. Chocolate lovers. Chocolate dream. Whatever you want to call it, this is the cake reserved exclusively for those passionate about chocolate. It's a moist chocolate cake loaded with chocolate chips, slathered in chocolate buttercream, and then topped with chocolate shavings. It would be a sin *not* to eat it!

PREP TIME: 20 minutes ◆ **BAKE TIME:** 30 to 35 minutes ◆ **SERVINGS:** 9

FOR THE CAKE
Nonstick baking spray
  (with flour)
1½ cups all-purpose flour
1 cup granulated sugar
½ cup unsweetened Dutch
  process cocoa powder
1 teaspoon baking soda
½ teaspoon salt
1 cup strong
  brewed coffee

½ cup coconut oil, melted
1 teaspoon vanilla extract
1 cup semisweet choco-
  late chips

FOR THE BUTTERCREAM
AND TOPPING

4 tablespoons (½ stick)
  unsalted butter, at room
  temperature
1 cup powdered
  sugar, sifted

¼ cup unsweetened
  Dutch process cocoa
  powder, sifted
1 to 3 teaspoons heavy
  (whipping) cream
½ teaspoon vanilla extract
Pinch of salt
1 (1.55-ounce) bar milk
  chocolate (such as
  Hershey's)

1. **Make the cake:** Preheat the oven to 350°F. Mist an 8-inch square baking pan with baking spray and line with a parchment sling (see page 9).

2. In a large bowl, whisk together the flour, granulated sugar, cocoa, baking soda, and salt. Add the coffee, coconut oil, and vanilla and mix until evenly combined. Fold in the chocolate chips.

3. Scrape the batter into the prepared pan. Bake for 30 to 35 minutes, until a toothpick inserted in the center of the cake comes out mostly clean.

4. Transfer the cake to a wire rack to cool for 10 minutes in the pan. Remove from the pan and set on the wire rack to cool completely. Discard the parchment and transfer to a serving plate.

5. **Meanwhile, make the buttercream:** In a large bowl, using an electric mixer on medium speed, beat the butter until light and fluffy. Add the powdered sugar, cocoa, 1 teaspoon of cream, and vanilla and beat until smooth. Add up to 2 additional teaspoons of cream until the frosting reaches your desired consistency.

6. Use an offset spatula to evenly frost the cooled cake with the buttercream. Slide the blade of a vegetable peeler across the smooth side of the chocolate bar to make chocolate curls. Use a toothpick or a clean offset spatula to lift the curls onto the frosted cake (don't use your hands; you'll melt the chocolate). Cut the cake into 9 squares to serve.

TOP IT OFF: Chocolate Ganache (page 126) can also be used instead of the buttercream.

INGREDIENT TIP: If you live in a humid climate like I do, pop your chocolate candy bar into the refrigerator prior to handling to prevent melting. You can also make the curls ahead and leave in the refrigerator until ready to use.

Chocolate-Glazed Pistachio Loaf • Page 90

Pecan Praline Cake

◆ MAKES 1 (8-INCH) SQUARE CAKE ◆

I love pralines. Perhaps it's because I was raised in the South, or perhaps it's because my grandmother always had different flavor offerings of the round, buttery, sugary melt-in-your-mouth pralines every Christmas. I love them so much I once adorned a cinnamon-based cookie with a praline, sprinkled it with some purple, green, and gold Mardi Gras colored sanding sugar, called it a Pecan Praline King Cake Cookie, and won myself a bake-off competition. This cake is devoted to that winning cookie combination, in cake form of course.

PREP TIME: 20 minutes ◆ **BAKE TIME:** 25 to 30 minutes ◆ **SERVINGS:** 9

FOR THE CAKE
Nonstick baking spray
  (with flour)
1½ cups all-purpose flour
1½ teaspoons
  baking powder
1 teaspoon ground
  cinnamon

¼ teaspoon salt
¾ cup granulated sugar
¼ cup coconut oil, melted
1 teaspoon vanilla extract
1 large egg
⅔ cup buttermilk

FOR THE TOPPING
¾ cup chopped pecans
½ cup packed light
  brown sugar
4 tablespoons (½ stick)
  unsalted butter, melted
2 tablespoons water
4 teaspoons
  all-purpose flour

1. **Make the cake:** Preheat the oven to 350°F. Mist an 8-inch square baking pan with baking spray and line with a parchment sling (see page 9).

2. In a medium bowl, combine the flour, baking powder, cinnamon, and salt.

3. In a large bowl, using an electric mixer on medium speed, beat together the granulated sugar, coconut oil, and vanilla. Beat in the egg. Add the flour mixture to the oil-sugar mixture, a little at a time and alternating with buttermilk, mixing well after each addition, until just combined.

4. Scrape the batter into the prepared baking pan. Bake for 25 to 30 minutes, until a toothpick inserted in the center of the cake comes out mostly clean.

5. Transfer the pan to a wire rack, but leave the oven on.

6. **Make the topping:** In a small bowl, mix together the pecans, brown sugar, melted butter, water, and flour and stir until well combined. Carefully spread the topping on top of the slightly cooled cake.

7. Return the cake to the oven and bake for an additional 10 minutes.

8. Transfer the pan to a wire rack to cool completely. Remove the cake from the pan, discard the parchment, and cut into 9 squares to serve.

White Chocolate Macadamia Nut Cake

◆ MAKES 1 (8-INCH) SQUARE CAKE ◆

The combination of mellow-sweet white chocolate with toothsome and buttery macadamias is a neo classic for a reason. If you like it in cookie form, then you'll go nuts over this cake. It is the ideal incarnation of the salty and sweet flavor.

PREP TIME: 20 minutes ◆ **BAKE TIME:** 30 to 35 minutes ◆ **SERVINGS:** 9

FOR THE CAKE
Nonstick baking spray
 (with flour)
1½ cups all-purpose flour
1 teaspoon
 baking powder
½ teaspoon salt
1 cup packed light
 brown sugar

8 tablespoons (1 stick)
 unsalted butter, at room
 temperature
1 large egg
1 cup buttermilk
1 teaspoon vanilla extract
1 cup white chocolate
 chips, divided

1 cup chopped salted
 dry-roasted macadamia
 nuts, divided

FOR THE TOPPING
½ cup all-purpose flour
½ cup packed light
 brown sugar
2 tablespoons unsalted
 butter, cubed

1. **Make the cake:** Preheat the oven to 350°F. Mist an 8-inch square baking pan with baking spray and line with a parchment sling (see page 9).

2. In a medium bowl, whisk together the flour, baking powder, and salt.

3. In a large bowl, with an electric mixer on medium speed, cream the brown sugar and butter for 2 to 3 minutes, until light and fluffy. Beat in the egg, buttermilk, and vanilla until well combined.

4. Add the flour mixture to the butter-sugar mixture, a little at a time, mixing to just combine. Fold in ½ cup of white chocolate chips and ½ cup of chopped macadamia nuts.

5. **Make the topping:** In a medium bowl, combine the flour and brown sugar. Using your fingers, a fork, or a pastry blender, cut in the butter until the mixture resembles coarse sand.

6. Scrape the batter into the prepared baking pan. Sprinkle the topping mixture on top of the batter, followed by the remaining ½ cup of white chocolate chips and ½ cup of nuts. Bake for 30 to 35 minutes, until a toothpick inserted in the center of the cake comes out mostly clean.

7. Transfer the pan to a wire rack to cool completely. Remove the cake from the pan, discard the parchment, and cut into 9 squares to serve.

....

TOP IT OFF: This cake has just enough sweetness with the chocolate chips added to the crumble topping, but a drizzle of Chocolate Ganache (page 126) can be added for extra oomph.

Chocolate-Glazed Pistachio Loaf

◆ MAKES 1 (8½-BY-4½-INCH) LOAF CAKE ◆

Nuts and chocolate are friends for a reason, and they work in almost any combination. I'm sure you've snacked on chocolate-covered almonds, but if you've never tried chocolate and pistachio, this cake is the perfect place to start. The deliciously rich pistachio pound cake is covered with a chocolate glaze and topped with roasted pistachios for good measure, and if you ask me, you should have it for breakfast.

PREP TIME: 20 minutes, plus 30 minutes to chill ◆ **BAKE TIME:** 55 minutes ◆
SERVINGS: 8

FOR THE CAKE
Nonstick baking spray
   (with flour)
2 cups all-purpose flour
½ cup finely ground salted
   roasted pistachios
½ teaspoon
   baking powder
½ teaspoon sea salt

1 cup (2 sticks) unsalted
   butter, at room
   temperature
1 cup granulated sugar
2 tablespoons honey
1½ teaspoons
   vanilla extract
½ teaspoon
   almond extract
3 large eggs
½ cup sour cream

FOR THE GLAZE
AND GARNISH

1 cup powdered sugar
3 tablespoons unsweet-
   ened Dutch process
   cocoa powder
2 tablespoons unsalted
   butter, melted
2 to 3 tablespoons
   hot water
¼ cup chopped salted
   roasted pistachios,
   for garnish

1. **Make the cake:** Preheat the oven to 325°F degrees. Mist an 8½-by-4½-inch loaf pan with baking spray and line the pan with a parchment sling (see page 9), with the overhang on the long sides.

2. In a medium bowl, whisk together the flour, ground pistachios, baking powder, and salt. Set aside.

3. In a large bowl, using an electric mixer on medium speed, cream together the butter and granulated sugar for 2 to 3 minutes, until light and fluffy. Beat in the honey, vanilla, and almond extract.

4. Add the eggs, one at a time, beating just until each egg is incorporated.

5. Add the flour mixture to the butter-sugar mixture, a little at a time and alternating with the sour cream, mixing well after each addition, until just combined.

6. Pour the batter into the prepared pan. Bake for 55 minutes to 1 hour, until the cake is golden brown and a toothpick inserted in the center of the cake comes out mostly clean.

7. Transfer the pan to a wire rack to cool completely.

8. **Make the glaze:** In a small bowl, combine the powdered sugar, cocoa, and melted butter. Add the hot water 1 tablespoon at a time, until the desired consistency is reached.

9. Pour the glaze over the cooled cake (still in the pan). While the glaze is still wet, sprinkle the chopped pistachios on top.

10. Refrigerate the cake for about 30 minutes to set the chocolate. Remove from the pan, discard the parchment paper, and cut into 8 slices to serve.

Toasted Butter Pecan Cake

◆ MAKES 1 (8-INCH) SQUARE CAKE ◆

Pecans gently toasted in butter give this super-simple cake a giant burst of flavor. It is reminiscent of butter pecan ice cream and is one of my most favorite cakes to make . . . and eat. Do yourself a favor and frost the cake with one of the suggested toppings, not because the cake needs it, but because you deserve to have your socks knocked off.

PREP TIME: 20 minutes ◆ **BAKE TIME:** 30 to 35 minutes ◆ **SERVINGS:** 9

Nonstick baking spray (with flour)
10 tablespoons (1¼ sticks) unsalted butter, divided
1 cup chopped pecans

1½ cups all-purpose flour
1 teaspoon baking powder
¼ teaspoon salt
1 cup sugar

1 teaspoon vanilla extract
2 large eggs
½ cup whole milk

1. Preheat the oven to 350°F. Mist an 8-inch square baking pan with baking spray and line with a parchment sling (see page 9).

2. In a small, heavy skillet, melt 2 tablespoons of butter over medium heat. Add the pecans and cook for about 4 minutes, or until toasted. Set aside to cool.

3. In a medium bowl, combine the flour, baking powder, and salt. Set aside.

4. In a large bowl, with an electric mixer on medium speed, cream the remaining 8 tablespoons of butter and the sugar for 2 to 3 minutes, until light and fluffy. Beat in the vanilla. Add the eggs, one at a time, beating just until each egg is incorporated.

5. Add the flour mixture to the butter-sugar mixture, a little at time and alternating with the milk, mixing well after each addition, until just combined. Fold in the buttered pecans.

6. Scrape the batter into the prepared baking pan. Bake for 30 to 35 minutes, until a toothpick inserted in the center of the cake comes out mostly clean.

7. Transfer the cake to a wire rack to cool for 10 minutes in the pan. Remove from the pan and set on the wire rack to cool completely. Discard the parchment and cut into 9 squares to serve.

TOP IT OFF: Small-Batch Vanilla Buttercream (page 132) will send this cake over the top, as will Cream Cheese Glaze (page 127). If you are going to frost the cake, set aside ¼ cup of the buttered pecans to use as a garnish and fold the remaining ¾ cup pecans into the batter as directed. Then after frosting the cake, sprinkle with the reserved buttered pecans.

Buttered Rum Cake

◆ MAKES 1 (8-INCH) SQUARE CAKE ◆

This cake is sweet and moist, while the toasted walnuts give it a bit of crunch. The extra rum sauce is so irresistible that you'll probably be caught licking the fork.

PREP TIME: 20 minutes ◆ **BAKE TIME:** 20 minutes ◆ **SERVINGS:** 9

FOR THE CAKE
Nonstick baking spray
(with flour)
8 tablespoons (1 stick)
unsalted butter, at room
temperature
½ cup packed light
brown sugar
2 tablespoons
granulated sugar
1 large egg

1½ tablespoons dark rum
1 teaspoon vanilla extract
1½ cups all-purpose flour
½ teaspoon
baking powder
¼ teaspoon baking soda
½ teaspoon ground
cinnamon
¼ teaspoon salt
⅓ cup chopped
toasted walnuts

FOR THE RUM SAUCE
½ cup packed light
brown sugar
4 tablespoons (½ stick)
unsalted butter
2 tablespoons heavy
(whipping) cream
1 tablespoon dark rum

1. **Make the cake:** Preheat the oven to 350°F. Mist an 8-inch square baking pan with baking spray and line with a parchment sling (see page 9).

2. In a small saucepan, heat the butter, brown sugar, and granulated sugar over medium heat, whisking occasionally for about 5 minutes, or until the butter is melted and the sugars are mostly dissolved. Allow the butter mixture to cool to room temperature so as not to scramble the egg in the upcoming step.

3. In a large bowl, whisk together the egg, rum, and vanilla. Whisk in the cooled butter mixture. Slowly add the flour, baking powder, baking soda, cinnamon, and salt, mixing to combine.

4. Scrape the batter into the prepared baking pan. Sprinkle the walnuts evenly over the top and press them lightly to adhere. Bake for 20 minutes, or until a toothpick inserted in the center of the cake comes out mostly clean.

5. Transfer the pan to a wire rack to cool slightly.

6. **Meanwhile, make the rum sauce:** In a small saucepan, combine the brown sugar, butter, cream, and rum and heat over medium heat, stirring occasionally, just until the butter is melted and the sugar is fully dissolved.

7. Prick holes in the top of the still-warm cake with a skewer or fork. Carefully pour the sauce over the top of the cake, allowing the sauce to seep into the holes.

8. Let the cake cool completely before removing from the pan. Discard the parchment paper and cut the cake into 9 squares to serve.

Peanut Butter Chocolate Chip Skillet Cake

◆ MAKES 1 (9-INCH) ROUND CAKE ◆

This cake has the perfect balance of nutty and sweet flavors, and an unparalleled texture. It's dense, moist, and delicious. Baking it in a cast-iron skillet ensures even baking, with both nice chewy edges and a gooey center.

PREP TIME: 15 minutes ◆ **BAKE TIME:** 45 minutes ◆ **SERVINGS:** 8

Nonstick baking spray (with flour)

¾ cup water

8 tablespoons (1 stick) unsalted butter, cubed

¾ cup sour cream

½ cup creamy peanut butter

1½ tablespoons vegetable oil

1 teaspoon vanilla extract

2 large eggs, lightly beaten

1½ cups all-purpose flour

½ cup granulated sugar

½ cup packed light brown sugar

1 teaspoon baking soda

¼ teaspoon baking powder

¼ teaspoon salt

1 cup semisweet chocolate chips

1. Preheat the oven to 350°F. Mist a 9-inch cast-iron skillet with baking spray and set aside.

2. In a microwave-safe medium bowl, microwave the water and butter on high for 1½ to 2 minutes, until the water is boiling. Add the sour cream, peanut butter, oil, and vanilla and whisk together until creamy. Whisk in the eggs just until combined.

3. In a large bowl, combine the flour, granulated and brown sugars, baking soda, baking powder, and salt. Add the peanut butter mixture and whisk until the batter is smooth.

4. Scrape the batter into the prepared skillet. Sprinkle the chocolate chips on top. Bake for 40 to 45 minutes, until a toothpick inserted in the center of the cake comes out mostly clean.

5. Let cool completely in the pan. Cut into 8 wedges and serve from the skillet.

Peanut Butter and Jelly Cake

◆ MAKES 1 (8-INCH) SQUARE CAKE ◆

This delicious cake gets its flavor combination from the familiar lunchtime staple, so it's perfect for including in lunch boxes as a sweet treat. Or have it for an afternoon snack or anytime you need something sweet but not too sweet. I've used blueberry jam, but you can use any jam you like.

PREP TIME: 20 minutes ◆ **BAKE TIME:** 25 to 30 minutes ◆ **SERVINGS:** 9

Nonstick baking spray
  (with flour)
1½ cups all-purpose flour
1 teaspoon
  baking powder
½ teaspoon baking soda

¼ teaspoon salt
8 tablespoons
  (1 stick) butter, at room
  temperature
¾ cup sugar

¼ cup creamy
  peanut butter
2 large eggs
½ cup whole milk
½ teaspoon vanilla extract
⅓ cup blueberry jam

1. Preheat the oven to 350°F. Mist an 8-inch square baking pan with baking spray and line with a parchment sling (see page 9).

2. In a medium bowl, whisk together the flour, baking powder, baking soda, and salt.

3. In large bowl, using an electric mixer on medium to high speed, cream the butter, sugar, and peanut butter together for 2 to 3 minutes, until light and fluffy. Add the eggs, one at time, beating just until each egg is incorporated.

4. In a small bowl, whisk together the milk and vanilla.

5. Add the flour mixture to the butter-sugar mixture, a little at a time and alternating with the milk-vanilla mixture, mixing well after each addition, until just combined.

6. Scrape the batter into the prepared baking pan. Add spoonfuls of jam to the top of the batter and run a knife through the jam to create swirls. Bake for 25 to 30 minutes, until a toothpick inserted in the center of the cake comes out mostly clean.

7. Transfer the cake to a wire rack to cool for 10 minutes in the pan. Remove from the pan and set on the wire rack to cool completely. Discard the parchment and cut the cake into 9 squares to serve.

Pecan Pie Cake

◆ MAKES 1 (8-INCH) SQUARE CAKE ◆

I am to pecan pie as Bubba in *Forrest Gump* was to shrimp. In my lifetime I've made pecan pie, bourbon pecan pie, chocolate chip pecan pie, sweet potato pecan pie, caramel apple pecan pie, bite-size pecan pies, pecan pie muffins . . . I'm sure you get the idea. It was only a matter of time before I transformed my beloved pecan pie into a snacking cake you can eat without utensils. You're welcome!

PREP TIME: 20 minutes ◆ **BAKE TIME:** 25 minutes ◆ **SERVINGS:** 9

FOR THE CAKE
Nonstick baking spray
  (with flour)
1½ cups all-purpose flour
½ teaspoon
  baking powder
½ teaspoon baking soda
¼ teaspoon salt

8 tablespoons (1 stick)
  unsalted butter
½ cup granulated sugar
2 large eggs
1 teaspoon vanilla extract
½ cup buttermilk
1 cup chopped pecans

FOR THE PECAN
PIE TOPPING
1 cup chopped pecans
½ cup light corn syrup
½ cup packed light
  brown sugar
3 tablespoons unsalted
  butter, melted
1 teaspoon vanilla extract

1. **Make the cake:** Preheat the oven to 350°F. Mist an 8-inch square baking pan with baking spray and line with a parchment sling (see page 9).

2. In a medium bowl, whisk together the flour, baking powder, baking soda, and salt. Set aside.

3. In a large bowl, with an electric mixer on medium speed, cream together the butter and granulated sugar for 2 to 3 minutes, until light and fluffy. Add the eggs, one at a time, beating until each egg is incorporated. Beat in the vanilla.

4. Add the flour mixture to the butter-sugar mixture, a little at time and alternating with the buttermilk, mixing well after each addition, until just combined. Fold in the pecans.

5. Scrape the batter into the prepared baking pan. Bake for 25 to 30 minutes, until a toothpick inserted in the center of the cake comes out mostly clean.

6. Transfer the cake to a wire rack to cool slightly.

7. **Meanwhile, make the pecan pie topping:** In a medium bowl, combine the pecans, corn syrup, brown sugar, melted butter, and vanilla and stir until smooth and the sugar is dissolved.

8. Prick holes in the top of the still-warm cake with a skewer or fork. Pour the topping over the top, allowing it to seep into the cake.

9. Allow the cake to cool completely in the pan. The topping will set up as the cake cools. Once cooled, remove the cake from the pan. Discard the parchment paper and cut the cake into 9 squares to serve.

TOP IT OFF: I always eat my pecan pie with a dollop of whipped cream or a scoop of ice cream. If you're the same, be sure to add a bit of Homemade Whipped Cream (page 130) or Brown Sugar Whipped Cream (page 130).

Peanut Butter Crunch Cake

◆ MAKES 1 (8-INCH) SQUARE CAKE ◆

Are you Team Smooth Peanut Butter or Team Crunchy? I am Team Crunchy, but my husband is Team Smooth. This cake combines the best of both worlds and isn't so crunchy that it'll scare off any smooth devotees. It's the ultimate peanut butter cake and will fill your kitchen with the most amazing aroma. Just be warned: If your pups typically get peanut butter as treats, they'll think you're baking something special for them!

PREP TIME: 20 minutes ◆ **BAKE TIME:** 25 minutes ◆ **SERVINGS:** 9

FOR THE CAKE
Nonstick baking spray
 (with flour)
1½ cups all-purpose flour
1 teaspoon
 baking powder
½ teaspoon baking soda
¼ teaspoon salt
¾ cup packed light
 brown sugar

8 tablespoons (1 stick)
 unsalted butter, at room
 temperature
¼ cup chunky
 peanut butter
2 large eggs
½ cup whole milk
½ teaspoon vanilla extract

FOR THE TOPPING
4 tablespoons (½ stick)
 unsalted butter
1 cup packed light
 brown sugar
½ cup whole milk
½ cup creamy
 peanut butter
½ cup chopped peanuts
½ teaspoon vanilla extract

1. **Make the cake:** Preheat the oven to 350°F. Mist an 8-inch square baking pan with baking spray and line with a parchment sling (see page 9).

2. In a medium bowl, whisk together the flour, baking powder, baking soda, and salt. Set aside.

3. In a large bowl, using an electric mixer on medium to high speed, cream the brown sugar, butter, and peanut butter together for 2 to 3 minutes, until light and fluffy. Add the eggs, one at time, beating until each egg is incorporated.

4. In a small bowl, whisk together the milk and vanilla.

5. Add the flour mixture to the butter-sugar mixture, a little at a time and alternating with the milk-vanilla mixture, mixing well after each addition, until just combined.

6. Scrape the batter into the prepared baking pan. Bake for 25 to 30 minutes, until a toothpick inserted in the center of the cake comes out mostly clean.

7. Transfer the pan to a wire rack to cool slightly. Prick holes in the top of the still-warm cake with a skewer or fork.

8. **Make the topping:** In a saucepan, melt the butter over medium heat. Stir in the brown sugar. Slowly add the milk and stir until the sugar dissolves. Bring to a boil and cook for about 5 minutes, or until the mixture thickens. Add the peanut butter and mix thoroughly. Remove from the heat, add the peanuts and vanilla, and stir until smooth. Allow the topping to cool to room temperature.

9. Pour the topping over the cake and let it set for 10 to 15 minutes. Remove the cake from the pan. Discard the parchment paper and cut the cake into 9 squares to serve.

Easy Almond Butter Cake

◆ MAKES 1 (8-INCH) SQUARE CAKE ◆

A snacking cake workhorse, a good almond cake is an essential part of any baker's repertoire. This one is more than typically delicious and is topped with an extra punch of almond butter sauce. Serving this cake is guaranteed to garner you rounds of high fives—but should you elect not to share with others, that is quite all right, too.

PREP TIME: 20 minutes ◆ **BAKE TIME:** 55 minutes ◆ **SERVINGS:** 9

FOR THE CAKE
Nonstick baking spray
   (with flour)
1½ cups all-purpose flour
½ teaspoon
   baking powder
½ teaspoon baking soda
½ teaspoon salt

8 tablespoons (1 stick)
   unsalted butter, at room
   temperature
1 cup sugar
2 large eggs
½ cup buttermilk
1 teaspoon almond extract

FOR THE SAUCE
AND GARNISH
½ cup sugar
4 tablespoons (½ stick)
   unsalted butter
2 tablespoons water
½ teaspoon
   almond extract
1 cup sliced almonds,
   for garnish

1. **Make the cake:** Preheat the oven to 350°F. Mist an 8-inch square baking pan with baking spray and line with a parchment paper (see page 9).

2. In a medium bowl, whisk together the flour, baking powder, baking soda, and salt. Set aside.

3. In a large bowl, using an electric mixer on medium speed, cream together the butter and sugar for 2 to 3 minutes, until light and fluffy. Add the eggs, one at a time, beating just until each egg is incorporated.

4. In a small bowl, combine the buttermilk and almond extract.

5. Add the flour mixture to the butter-sugar mixture, a little at a time and alternating with the buttermilk mixture, mixing well after each addition, until just combined.

6. Scrape the batter into the prepared baking pan. Bake for about 55 minutes, or until a toothpick inserted in the center of the cake comes out mostly clean.

7. Transfer the pan to a wire rack to cool slightly.

8. **Meanwhile, make the sauce:** In a small saucepan, bring the sugar, butter, and water to a low boil, stirring to dissolve the sugar. Remove from the heat and stir in the almond extract.

9. Prick holes in the top of the still-warm cake with a skewer or fork. Pour the butter sauce over the cake, allowing the sauce to seep into the holes. Cover the cake with the sliced almonds.

10. Allow the cake to cool for an additional 10 minutes in the pan, then remove it from the pan and set the cake on the wire rack to cool completely. Discard the parchment and cut the cake into 9 squares to serve.

Honey Walnut Cake

◆ MAKES 1 (8-INCH) SQUARE CAKE ◆

Walnuts, spices, and honey is a combination made in snacking-cake heaven. This delicious little honey-flavored, spice-filled cake makes for incredible afternoon snacking when you need an instant boost of energy to combat that midday slump. It's all thanks to a double helping of honey: in the batter and in the nutty filling.

PREP TIME: 20 minutes ◆ **BAKE TIME:** 35 to 40 minutes ◆ **SERVINGS:** 9

FOR THE CAKE
Nonstick baking spray
(with flour)
1½ cups all-purpose flour
½ teaspoon
baking powder
½ teaspoon baking soda
½ teaspoon salt
½ teaspoon ground
cinnamon

½ teaspoon
ground nutmeg
8 tablespoons (1 stick)
unsalted butter, at room
temperature
¼ cup packed light
brown sugar
½ cup honey
1 large egg
½ cup sour cream
1 teaspoon vanilla extract

FOR THE FILLING
1 cup chopped walnuts
2 tablespoons honey
2 tablespoons light
brown sugar
1 teaspoon ground
cinnamon

1. **Make the cake:** Preheat the oven to 350°F. Mist an 8-inch square baking pan with baking spray and line with a parchment sling (see page 9).

2. In a large bowl, whisk together the flour, baking powder, baking soda, salt, cinnamon, and nutmeg. Set aside.

3. In a large bowl, using an electric mixer on medium speed, cream together the butter and brown sugar for 2 to 3 minutes, until light and fluffy. Add the honey and beat until smooth. Beat in the egg, sour cream, and vanilla until well combined.

4. Add the flour mixture to the butter-sugar mixture, a little at a time, mixing after each addition, until just combined.

5. **Make the filling:** In a medium bowl, mix together the walnuts, honey, brown sugar, and cinnamon until smooth.

6. Pour half of the batter into the prepared baking pan. Top with the honey-nut filling. Scrape in the remaining batter to cover. Bake for 35 to 40 minutes, until a toothpick inserted in the center of the cake comes out mostly clean.

7. Transfer the cake to a wire rack to cool for 10 minutes in the pan. Remove from the pan and set on the wire rack to cool completely. Discard the parchment and cut the cake into 9 squares to serve.

TOP IT OFF: Honey Glaze (page 129) takes this cake from great to extraordinary. Bonus: It's a third helping of honey!

Nutty Caramel Cake

◆ MAKES 1 (8-INCH) SQUARE CAKE ◆

My grandmother would often declare she was allergic to nuts, yet she also loved serving this cake. I even caught her indulging one time, and when I reminded her of her allergy, she explained, "Aimee, I tell the neighbors that so they'd stop bringing me fruit cakes during the holidays." Lucky for us, this cake remained despite her neighborhood fibbing.

PREP TIME: 20 minutes ◆ **BAKE TIME:** 20 to 25 minutes ◆ **SERVINGS:** 9

Nonstick baking spray
  (with flour)
1½ cups all-purpose flour
1½ teaspoons
  baking powder
¼ teaspoon salt

8 tablespoons (1 stick)
  unsalted butter, at room
  temperature
1 cup packed light
  brown sugar

2 large eggs
½ cup whole milk
1 teaspoon vanilla extract
1 cup chopped pecans

1. Preheat the oven to 350°F. Mist an 8-inch square baking pan with baking spray and line with a parchment sling (see page 9).

2. In a medium bowl, whisk together the flour, baking powder, and salt. Set aside.

3. In a large bowl, with an electric mixer on medium speed, cream together the butter and brown sugar for 2 to 3 minutes, until light and fluffy. Add the eggs, one at a time, beating just until each egg is incorporated.

4. In a small bowl, stir together the milk and vanilla.

5. Add the flour mixture to the butter-sugar mixture, a little at a time and alternating with the milk-vanilla mixture, mixing until just combined. Fold in the chopped pecans.

6. Scrape the batter into the prepared baking pan. Bake for 20 to 25 minutes, until a toothpick inserted in the center of the cake comes out mostly clean.

7. Transfer the cake to a wire rack to cool for about 10 minutes in the pan. Remove from the pan and set on the wire rack to cool completely. Discard the parchment and cut the cake into 9 squares to serve.

Butterscotch Pecan Cake

◆ MAKES 1 (8-INCH) SQUARE CAKE ◆

This cake pays homage to my grandmother Jeanne's creamy, nutty, and delicious butterscotch pralines. I had to teach myself how to make them once I moved beyond a reasonable driving distance from my grandmother . . . and now I've gone and turned her butterscotch pralines into a cake.

PREP TIME: 20 minutes ◆ **BAKE TIME:** 30 to 35 minutes ◆ **SERVINGS:** 9

Nonstick baking spray
  (with flour)
1½ cups all-purpose flour
1 (3.4-ounce) box butter-
  scotch instant pudding
1½ teaspoons
  baking powder

¼ teaspoon salt
8 tablespoons (1 stick)
  unsalted butter, at room
  temperature
1 cup packed light
  brown sugar

3 large eggs
1 teaspoon vanilla extract
1 cup buttermilk
1 cup chopped pecans
½ cup butterscotch chips

1. Preheat the oven to 350°F. Mist an 8-inch square baking pan with baking spray and line with a parchment sling (see page 9).

2. In a medium bowl, whisk together the flour, pudding mix, baking powder, and salt.

3. In a large bowl, using an electric mixer on medium speed, cream together the butter and brown sugar for 2 to 3 minutes, until light and fluffy. Add the eggs, one at a time, beating until each egg is incorporated. Beat in the vanilla.

4. Add the flour mixture to the butter-sugar mixture, a little a time and alternating with the buttermilk, mixing well after each addition, until just combined. Fold in the pecans and butterscotch chips.

5. Scrape the batter into the prepared baking pan. Bake for 30 to 35 minutes, until a toothpick inserted in the center of the cake comes out mostly clean.

6. Transfer the cake to a wire rack to cool for 10 minutes in the pan. Remove from the pan and set on the wire rack to cool completely. Discard the parchment and cut the cake into 9 squares to serve.

Nutrageous Upside-Down Cake

◆ MAKES 1 (8-INCH) ROUND CAKE ◆

I call this cake my accident cake. It gets its double dose of nuts not because I was being overly creative, but because the recipe called for pecans, and I didn't quite have a full cup of pecans. I could've used the full amount of walnuts, but because both nuts pair so well with maple, I decided to combine them. The result was so delicious that I never looked back.

PREP TIME: 20 minutes ◆ **BAKE TIME:** 35 to 40 minutes ◆ **SERVINGS:** 8

8 tablespoons (1 stick) unsalted butter, at room temperature, plus more for the pan

1 cup maple syrup

½ chopped pecans

½ cup chopped walnuts

1½ cups all-purpose flour

1½ teaspoons baking powder

1 teaspoon salt

¾ cup sugar

2 large eggs

1 teaspoon vanilla extract

½ teaspoon maple extract

⅔ cup buttermilk

1. Preheat the oven to 350°F. Generously butter an 8-inch round cake pan.

2. Pour the maple syrup into the prepared pan and cover with the nuts.

3. In a medium bowl, whisk together the flour, baking powder, and salt. Set aside.

4. In a large bowl, using an electric mixer on medium speed, cream the butter and sugar together for 2 to 3 minutes, until light and fluffy.

5. Add the eggs, one at a time, beating just until each egg is incorporated. Beat in the vanilla and maple extract.

6. Add the flour mixture to the butter-sugar mixture, a little at a time and alternating with the buttermilk, mixing well after each addition, until just combined.

7. Scrape the batter into the prepared baking pan. Use an offset spatula to spread the batter evenly over the nuts. Bake for 35 to 40 minutes, until a toothpick inserted in the center of the cake comes out mostly clean.

8. Transfer the cake to a wire rack to cool for 10 minutes in the pan. Run a knife or cake release tool around the edges of the pan and invert the cake onto a serving plate, nut-side up. Cut the cake into 8 slices to serve.

TOP IT OFF: This cake pairs well with a drizzle of Maple Glaze (page 129) just before serving or alongside a scoop of vanilla ice cream.

Confetti Birthday Cake • Page 116

One-Bowl Chocolate Fudge Cake

VEGAN • MAKES 1 (8-INCH) ROUND CAKE •

Rich and indulgent, this cake comes together quickly with just one bowl and pantry ingredients, making it the perfect recipe for when those sudden chocolate cravings arise. Its intense chocolate flavor comes from the addition of cold coffee, but don't let that deter you: The cake tastes nothing like coffee, just even more chocolaty.

PREP TIME: 10 minutes • **BAKE TIME:** 30 minutes • **SERVINGS:** 8

Nonstick baking spray
   (with flour)
1¼ cups all-purpose flour
1 cup sugar
½ cup unsweetened Dutch
   process cocoa powder

1 teaspoon baking soda
½ teaspoon salt
1 cup brewed coffee, at
   room temperature

¼ cup coconut oil, melted
1 teaspoon vanilla extract
1 cup vegan chocolate
   chips (optional)

1. Preheat the oven to 350°F. Mist an 8-inch round cake pan with baking spray and line the bottom with a round of parchment paper.

2. In a large bowl, whisk together the flour, sugar, cocoa, baking soda, and salt. Stir in the coffee, coconut oil, and vanilla just until combined. Fold in the chocolate chips (if using).

3. Scrape the batter into the prepared cake pan. Bake for 25 to 30 minutes, until the middle of the cake is set and a toothpick inserted in the center comes out mostly clean.

4. Transfer the pan to a wire rack to cool completely. Use a cake release tool or a knife and run along the sides of the cake to loosen. Then remove from the pan, discard the parchment paper, and cut into 8 slices to serve.

TOP IT OFF: This cake is delicious on its own, but a simple dusting of powdered sugar never hurt. If you are not vegan (but are a chocolate lover), top it with Chocolate Ganache (page 126). Homemade Whipped Cream (page 130) or Vegan Coconut Whip (page 131) would balance some of the richness.

SUBSTITUTION: Water can be used in place of coffee if the thought of adding coffee is not up your alley.

Gingerbread Cake

 ◆ MAKES 1 (8-INCH) SQUARE CAKE ◆

Gingerbread cookies are synonymous with the holidays, and now you can enjoy the cookie nostalgia in a small-batch cake anytime of the year. This cake is moist, tender, and packed with ultracomforting spiced gingerbread-flavored goodness. Bring on the caroling—or not!

PREP TIME: 10 minutes ◆ **BAKE TIME:** 45 minutes ◆ **SERVINGS:** 9

Nonstick baking spray (with flour)
1½ cups all-purpose flour
½ teaspoon ground cardamom
½ teaspoon ground cinnamon
½ teaspoon ground cloves
½ teaspoon baking powder
¼ teaspoon salt
½ cup coconut oil, melted
¾ cup packed light brown sugar
½ cup molasses
½ cup unsweetened applesauce

1. Preheat the oven to 350°F. Mist an 8-inch square baking pan with baking spray and line with a parchment sling (see page 9).

2. In a medium bowl, whisk together the flour, cardamom, cinnamon, cloves, baking powder, and salt. Set aside.

3. In a large bowl, using an electric mixer on medium speed, beat the coconut oil, brown sugar, molasses, and applesauce together for about 2 minutes, until well combined.

4. Add the flour mixture to the coconut oil–sugar mixture, a little at a time, beating until just combined.

5. Scrape the batter into the prepared baking pan. Bake for about 45 minutes, or until a toothpick inserted in the center of the cake comes out mostly clean.

6. Transfer the pan to a wire rack to cool completely. Remove the cake from the pan, discard the parchment, and cut into 9 squares to serve.

TOP IT OFF: A dusting of powdered sugar is all this classic cake needs.

Strawberry Lemonade Cake

VEGAN ◆ MAKES 1 (8-INCH) SQUARE CAKE ◆

This cake tastes like pure summertime. Light and fruity, the subtle lemon cake is covered with an extra generous strawberry topping. It's perfect for weekend barbecues when you don't want a lot of leftover dessert. Since good strawberries are typically available year-round, use fresh, since the topping is such a key player in this cake.

PREP TIME: 20 minutes ◆ **BAKE TIME:** 30 minutes ◆ **SERVINGS:** 9

FOR THE CAKE
Nonstick baking spray
  (with flour)
1½ cups all-purpose flour
¾ cup sugar
1 teaspoon baking soda
½ teaspoon
  baking powder
¼ teaspoon salt

½ cup vegetable oil
½ cup canned full-fat
  coconut milk
⅓ cup sweetened
  applesauce
Grated zest of 1 lemon
2 tablespoons fresh
  lemon juice
½ teaspoon vanilla extract

FOR THE TOPPING
2 cups strawberries
  (16 ounces), hulled
  and sliced
½ cup sugar
¼ cup water
2 tablespoons cornstarch

1. **Make the cake:** Preheat the oven to 350°F. Mist an 8-inch square baking pan with baking spray and line with a parchment sling (see page 9).

2. In a large bowl, whisk together the flour, sugar, baking soda, baking powder, and salt. Add the oil, coconut milk, applesauce, lemon zest, lemon juice, and vanilla. Mix just until combined and the flour has disappeared.

3. Scrape the batter into the prepared baking pan. Bake for about 30 minutes, or until a toothpick inserted in the center of the cake comes out mostly clean.

4. Transfer the pan to a wire rack to cool completely.

5. **Make the topping:** In a medium saucepan, combine the strawberries, sugar, water, and cornstarch. Cook over medium-high heat for about 5 minutes, or until the sauce boils and thickens.

6. Spread the topping over the cooled cake and let the topping set for at least 10 minutes. Remove the cake from the pan, discard the parchment, and cut into 9 squares to serve.

Confetti Birthday Cake

GLUTEN FREE ◆ MAKES 1 (8-INCH) ROUND CAKE ◆

Is there anything more fun than a cake with sprinkles? This homemade version of the beloved box mix is delicious, easy, and fun to make. It's perfect for gifting, too. Just grab a disposable cake container, load it with precut cake slices, and tie it up with ribbon. It is certain to bring a smile to someone's face.

PREP TIME: 10 minutes ◆ **BAKE TIME:** 30 minutes ◆ **SERVINGS:** 9

FOR THE CAKE
Butter, for the pan
1½ cups 1:1 gluten-free all-purpose flour
¾ cup granulated sugar
1½ teaspoons baking powder
½ teaspoon salt
½ cup whole milk
½ cup vegetable oil

2 large eggs
1 teaspoon vanilla extract
½ teaspoon almond extract
⅓ cup rainbow sprinkles

FOR THE FROSTING AND TOPPING
4 tablespoons (½ stick) unsalted butter, at room temperature

1 cup powdered sugar, sifted
1 to 3 teaspoons heavy (whipping) cream
½ teaspoon vanilla extract
Rainbow sprinkles, for topping

1. **Make the cake:** Preheat the oven to 350°F. Mist an 8-inch round cake pan with baking spray and line the bottom with a round of parchment paper.

2. In a medium bowl, whisk together the gluten-free flour, granulated sugar, baking powder, and salt. Add the milk, oil, eggs, vanilla, and almond extract and mix until combined. Fold in the sprinkles.

3. Scrape the batter into the prepared baking pan. Bake for about 30 minutes, or until a toothpick inserted in the center of the cake comes out mostly clean.

4. Transfer the cake to a wire rack to cool for 10 minutes in the pan. Remove from the pan and set on the wire rack to cool completely before frosting. Discard the parchment.

5. **Make the frosting:** In a medium bowl, using an electric mixer on medium speed, cream the butter for 1 to 2 minutes, until light and fluffy. Add the powdered sugar, 1 teaspoon of cream, and the vanilla and beat until smooth. Add up to 2 additional teaspoons of cream until the frosting reaches the desired consistency and is easily spreadable.

6. Once the cake has cooled completely, use an offset spatula to frost the top of the cake. Sprinkle with rainbow sprinkles. Cut the cake into 9 slices to serve.

INGREDIENT TIP: Use the longer rather than shorter sprinkles because they will keep their color and not bleed into the batter as much as shorter sprinkles.

Oatmeal Raisin Carrot Cake

GLUTEN FREE ◆ MAKES 1 (8-INCH) SQUARE CAKE ◆

This cake came into the world one Easter when it was just my husband
and me and it seemed silly to whip up a three-layer carrot cake for the two of us.
Should you find yourself with leftovers, it also does double duty as breakfast
thanks to the addition of oatmeal.

PREP TIME: 10 minutes ◆ **BAKE TIME:** 35 to 40 minutes ◆ **SERVINGS:** 9

Butter, for the pan

1 cup almond flour

1 cup gluten-free
quick-cooking oats

1 teaspoon baking soda

1 teaspoon ground
cinnamon

½ teaspoon
ground nutmeg

8 tablespoons (1 stick)
unsalted butter, at room
temperature

½ cup sugar

1 large egg

⅓ cup maple syrup

½ cup grated carrots

⅓ cup raisins

1. Preheat the oven to 350°F. Coat an 8-inch square baking pan with butter and line
   with a parchment sling (see page 9).

2. In a large bowl, whisk together the almond flour, oats, baking soda, cinnamon,
   and nutmeg. Set aside.

3. In a large bowl, using an electric mixer on medium speed, cream the butter and
   sugar together for 2 to 3 minutes, until light and fluffy. Beat in the egg and maple
   syrup. Add the flour mixture to the butter-sugar mixture a little at a time, mixing
   well after each addition, until just combine. Fold in the carrots and raisins.

4. Scrape the batter into the prepared pan. Bake for 35 to 40 minutes, until the top is
   golden brown and a toothpick inserted in the center of the cake comes out clean.

5. Transfer the pan to a wire rack to cool completely. Remove the cake from the pan,
   discard the parchment, and cut into 9 squares to serve.

SUBSTITUTION: To make this vegan, use coconut oil to grease the pan and use ¼ cup of applesauce in
place of the egg and almond butter in place of the dairy butter.

Banana Chocolate Chip Cake

GLUTEN FREE ✦ MAKES 1 (8-INCH) SQUARE CAKE ✦

This cake is light and moist, and makes for the perfect use of ripe bananas when you're in the mood for something a little more special than plain ole banana bread. It can stand alone just fine without the mini chocolate chips, but I like to add them for additional flavor and texture; a little goes a long way.

PREP TIME: 20 minutes ✦ **BAKE TIME:** 25 minutes ✦ **SERVINGS:** 9

Butter, for the pan
1¾ cups 1:1 gluten-free all-purpose flour
1 teaspoon ground cinnamon
1 teaspoon baking soda
½ teaspoon baking powder

¼ teaspoon salt
8 tablespoons (1 stick) unsalted butter, at room temperature
¾ cup packed light brown sugar
½ cup whole milk
2 large eggs

1½ teaspoons vanilla extract
1 cup mashed bananas (about 3 bananas)
½ cup mini chocolate chips

1. Preheat the oven to 350°F. Coat an 8-inch square baking pan with butter and line with a parchment sling (see page 9).

2. In a medium bowl, whisk together the gluten-free flour, cinnamon, baking soda, baking powder, and salt. Set aside.

3. In a large bowl, using an electric mixer on medium speed, cream the butter and brown sugar together for 2 to 3 minutes, until light and fluffy. Add the milk, eggs, and vanilla, mixing until well combined.

4. Add the flour mixture, a little at a time, to the butter-sugar mixture, mixing until just combined. Fold in the mashed bananas and mini chocolate chips.

5. Scrape the batter into the prepared baking pan. Bake for 22 to 25 minutes, until a toothpick inserted in the center of the cake comes out mostly clean.

6. Transfer the pan to a wire rack to cool completely. Remove the cake from the pan, discard the parchment, and cut into 9 squares to serve.

Pineapple Upside-Down Cake

VEGAN **GLUTEN FREE** ◆ MAKES 1 (8-INCH) ROUND CAKE ◆

Made with a moist coconut milk batter and topped with pineapple slices, maraschino cherries, and caramelized brown sugar, this childhood classic gets a makeover by making it both gluten-free and vegan friendly. It's so delicious, no one will even know there were substitutions.

PREP TIME: 20 minutes ◆ **BAKE TIME:** 45 minutes ◆ **SERVINGS:** 8

2 tablespoons coconut oil

2 tablespoons light
   brown sugar

8 juice-packed canned
   pineapple rings, drained
   (liquid reserved)

8 maraschino cherries,
   without stems

1½ cups 1:1 gluten-free
   all-purpose flour

¾ cup granulated sugar

1 teaspoon
   baking powder

½ teaspoon baking soda

¼ teaspoon salt

½ cup canned full-fat
   coconut milk

⅓ cup pineapple juice
   (liquid from the can)

⅓ cup unsweetened
   applesauce

1. Preheat the oven to 350°F. Place the coconut oil in the bottom of an 8-inch round cake pan and place into the preheated oven to melt.

2. Remove the pan from the oven and sprinkle the brown sugar over the melted oil, covering the entire pan. Arrange the pineapple slices on top of the brown sugar and place a cherry in the center of each pineapple ring.

3. In a large bowl, whisk together the gluten-free flour, granulated sugar, baking powder, baking soda, and salt. Add the coconut milk, pineapple juice, and applesauce and mix well.

4. Slowly pour the batter (so as not to disturb the cherries) into the baking pan over the pineapple slices. Bake for about 45 minutes, or until a toothpick inserted in the center of the cake comes out mostly clean.

5. Transfer the cake to a wire rack to cool for 10 minutes in the pan. Loosen the cake with a knife or cake release tool and place a serving plate or cake stand upside down over the cake pan. Flip the plate and pan together and slowly remove the baking pan. Allow the cake to finish cooling completely before serving. Cut the cake into 8 slices to serve.

INGREDIENT TIP: Using a paper towel to blot excess liquid from the jarred cherries will keep your cake topping from turning red.

SUBSTITUTION: Vegan butter can be used instead of coconut oil for the pineapple topping if you have it on hand.

Salted Caramel Apple Cake

VEGAN GLUTEN FREE ◆ MAKES 1 (8-INCH) SQUARE CAKE ◆

Caramel and apples go together like peanut butter and jelly, and there is no better time to marry the two than when the fall temperatures begin to drop. Cozy up with this cake after a chilly hayride or use it for a well-deserved treat following an afternoon of raking leaves.

PREP TIME: 20 minutes ◆ **BAKE TIME:** 30 to 35 minutes ◆ **SERVINGS:** 9

FOR THE CAKE
Coconut oil, for the pan
1¾ cups 1:1 gluten-free
    all-purpose flour
½ cup packed light
    brown sugar
½ cup granulated sugar
½ teaspoon
    baking powder

½ teaspoon baking soda
½ cup unsweetened
    applesauce
½ cup canned full-fat
    coconut milk
1 teaspoon vanilla extract
2 cups diced peeled
    apples (about
    2 medium apples)

FOR THE SAUCE
½ cup canned
    coconut cream
½ cup packed light
    brown sugar
1½ teaspoons cornstarch
1 teaspoon coarse sea salt

1. **Make the cake:** Preheat the oven to 350°F. Coat an 8-inch square baking pan with coconut oil and line with a parchment sling (see page 9).

2. In a large bowl, whisk together the gluten-free flour, brown and granulated sugars, baking powder, salt, and baking soda. Whisk in the applesauce, coconut milk, and vanilla until combined. Fold in the diced apples.

3. Scrape the batter into the prepared baking pan. Bake for 30 to 35 minutes, until a toothpick inserted in the center of the cake comes out mostly clean.

4. Transfer the pan to a wire rack to cool completely.

5. **Meanwhile, make the sauce:** In a small saucepan, whisk together the coconut cream, brown sugar, and cornstarch over medium-high heat, stirring constantly while the coconut cream melts. Stir in the salt. Reduce the heat and simmer for about 5 minutes. Allow the sauce to cool slightly.

6. Prick holes in the top of the cake with a skewer or folk. Pour half of the sauce over the cake. Allow the caramel to set for about 10 minutes. Remove the cake from the pan, discard the parchment, and transfer the cake to a serving platter. Cut the cake into 9 squares to serve. Drizzling some of the remaining sauce over each serving.

TOP IT OFF: This cake is phenomenal with a scoop of vegan ice cream topped with the caramel sauce, or a dollop of Vegan Coconut Whip (page 131).

Pecan Caramel Sauce • Page 134

Toppings

Chocolate Ganache

With only two ingredients, this topper is both creamy and chocolaty. It can have a pourable consistency (great for glazing) or a spreadable consistency—the choice is all yours.

PREP TIME: 5 minutes   ◆   **MAKES:** 1½ cups

1 cup chocolate chips
(milk, semisweet,
bittersweet—your choice)

½ cup heavy
(whipping) cream

1. In a microwave-safe medium bowl, microwave the chocolate chips and cream in 30-second intervals, stirring after each. Continue microwaving until the ganache is thick and smooth.

2. Use right away to drizzle over a cake or let it set up at room temperature for several hours until it's spreadable.

STORAGE: Will keep covered with plastic wrap in the refrigerator for up to 2 days.

◈ **Chocolate Peanut Butter Ganache:** Follow the directions using ½ cup of semisweet chocolate chips, ½ cup of peanut butter chips, and ½ cup of heavy (whipping) cream.

◈ **Mexican Chocolate Ganache:** Follow the directions using 1 cup of semisweet chocolate chips and ½ cup of heavy (whipping) cream. When the ganache is thick and smooth, stir in ¼ teaspoon of ground cinnamon and ¼ teaspoon of cayenne pepper.

◈ **Mint Chocolate Ganache:** Follow the directions using 1 cup of semisweet chocolate chips and ½ cup of heavy (whipping) cream. When the ganache is thick and smooth, stir in ¼ teaspoon of peppermint extract.

◈ **White Chocolate Ganache:** Follow the directions, but swap out the chocolate chips for white chocolate chips.

Cream Cheese Glaze

Effortless and delicious, this tangy topping is a perfect addition to just about any cake, but especially delectable on a crumb-topped coffee cake.

PREP TIME: 5 minutes ◆ **MAKES:** ¾ cup

1 cup powdered sugar

4 ounces cream cheese, at room temperature

¼ cup whole milk
1 teaspoon vanilla extract

1. In a large bowl, using an electric mixer on medium speed, beat the powdered sugar and cream cheese together until fully combined.

2. On low speed, beat in the milk and vanilla until the milk is worked into the glaze.

3. Use a spoon to drizzle the glaze or, for more coverage, pour directly on top of the cake. Allow the glaze to set before serving.

STORAGE: Will keep covered with plastic wrap in the refrigerator for 2 to 3 days.

Peanut Butter Glaze

This glaze pairs particularly well with any cake that has chocolate in it, but especially the Lagniappe Cake (page 74) when made with peanut butter cups.

PREP TIME: 5 minutes ◆ **MAKES:** 1 cup

¼ cup creamy
  peanut butter

2 tablespoons
  unsalted butter

6 tablespoons whole milk

¼ teaspoon vanilla extract

1 ¼ cups powdered sugar

1. In a microwave-safe medium bowl, microwave the peanut butter and butter until melted, about 30 seconds. Whisk until smooth. Whisk in the milk and vanilla. Whisk in the powdered sugar until smooth.

2. Use a spoon to drizzle the glaze or, for more coverage, pour directly on top of the cake. Allow the glaze to set before serving.

STORAGE: Will keep covered with plastic wrap in the refrigerator for 6 to 7 days.

Vanilla Glaze

This is a great little topping for any cake. It is simple to put together, and adds a nice amount of sweetness and another dimension of flavor to finish the dessert.

PREP TIME: 2 minutes ◆ **MAKES:** ¾ cup

1 cup powdered sugar

3 tablespoons heavy (whipping) cream

1 teaspoon vanilla extract

1. In a medium bowl, whisk the powdered sugar, cream, and vanilla together until smooth.

2. Drizzle the glaze on top of the cake.

STORAGE: Will keep covered with plastic wrap in the refrigerator for 6 to 7 days.

◈ **Cinnamon Glaze:** Follow the directions using 1 cup of powdered sugar, 2 tablespoons of heavy (whipping) cream, ½ teaspoon of vanilla extract, and 1 teaspoon of ground cinnamon.

◈ **Coffee Glaze:** Follow the directions using 1 cup of powdered sugar and 1½ tablespoons of strongly brewed coffee.

◈ **Honey Glaze:** Follow the directions using 1 cup of powdered sugar, 2 tablespoons of honey, 2 tablespoons of heavy (whipping) cream, and ½ teaspoon of vanilla extract.

◈ **Lemon Glaze:** Follow the directions using ¾ cup of powdered sugar, the grated zest of 1 lemon, and 2 tablespoons of fresh lemon juice.

◈ **Maple Glaze:** Follow the directions using 1 cup of powdered sugar, 3 tablespoons of heavy (whipping) cream, and 1 teaspoon of maple extract.

◈ **Maraschino Cherry Glaze:** Follow the directions using ¾ cup of powdered sugar and 2 tablespoons of juice from a jar of maraschino cherries.

Homemade Whipped Cream

Whipped cream is always best when it's homemade, and this light, barely-there topping works with any flavor cake.

PREP TIME: 5 minutes ◆ **MAKES:** 2 cups

1 cup heavy (whipping) cream, chilled

1 tablespoon powdered sugar

½ teaspoon vanilla extract

In a bowl, using an electric mixer on medium speed, beat the cream, powdered sugar, and vanilla together for about 5 minutes, or until stiff peaks form. Use immediately.

◈ **Brown Sugar Whipped Cream:** Follow the directions using 1 cup of heavy (whipping) cream and 2 tablespoons of light brown sugar.

◈ **Chocolate Whipped Cream:** Follow the directions using 1 cup of heavy (whipping) cream, 2 tablespoons of sifted unsweetened cocoa powder, and 4 teaspoons of granulated sugar.

Vegan Coconut Whip

This dairy-free whipped topping is easy to make at home and adds a special something to cakes that pair well with the rich taste of coconut.

PREP TIME: 5 minutes ◆ **MAKES:** 2 cups

1 (13.5-ounce) can coconut cream

2 tablespoons powdered sugar, sifted, or more to taste

¼ teaspoon coconut extract

1. Refrigerate the can of coconut cream overnight.

2. Once the coconut cream is cold, open the can and transfer only the thick and creamy part to the bowl. Discard any liquid at the bottom of the can.

3. In a bowl, using an electric mixer on medium speed, beat the coconut cream, powdered sugar, and coconut extract together for 2 to 3 minutes, until stiff peaks form. Use immediately.

Small-Batch Vanilla Buttercream

I developed this recipe for a classic American vanilla frosting to be just the right-size batch for a snacking cake. It's the perfect topper for celebration cakes.

PREP TIME: 5 minutes ◆ **MAKES:** ¾ cup

4 tablespoons (½ stick) unsalted butter, at room temperature

1 cup powdered sugar, sifted

1½ to 3 teaspoons heavy (whipping) cream
½ teaspoon vanilla extract

In a bowl, using an electric mixer on medium speed, beat the butter for 2 to 3 minutes, until light and fluffy. Add the powdered sugar, 1½ teaspoons of cream, and vanilla and beat until smooth. Add the remaining 1½ teaspoons of cream as needed, in ½-teaspoon increments, until the frosting reaches your desired consistency.

STORAGE: If not using right away, gently press plastic wrap directly on top of the frosting to prevent a skin from forming. Store at room temperature for 2 to 3 days.

Small-Batch Chocolate Buttercream

Rich and creamy, this topping is the ultimate exclamation point on any of the chocolate cakes, but is necessary (in my opinion) for the classic birthday yellow cake/chocolate frosting combination.

PREP TIME: 5 minutes ◆ **MAKES:** ¾ cup

4 tablespoons (½ stick) unsalted butter, at room temperature

1 cup powdered sugar, sifted

¼ cup unsweetened Dutch process cocoa powder, sifted

Pinch salt

1½ teaspoons to 3 teaspoons heavy (whipping) cream

½ teaspoon vanilla extract

In a bowl, using an electric mixer on medium speed, beat the butter for 2 to 3 minutes, until light and fluffy. Add the powdered sugar, cocoa powder, salt, 1½ teaspoons of cream, and vanilla and beat until smooth. Add the remaining 1½ teaspoons of cream as needed, in ½-teaspoon increments, until the frosting reaches your desired consistency.

STORAGE: If not using right away, gently press the plastic wrap directly on top of the frosting to prevent a skin from forming. Store at room temperature for 2 to 3 days.

Pecan Caramel Sauce

This topping is especially delicious on any of the cakes you want to add a bit of pizazz to but also serves as last-minute drizzle finales.

PREP TIME: 5 minutes ◆ **MAKES:** 1 cup

½ cup packed light brown sugar

½ cup heavy (whipping) cream

1 teaspoon salt

¾ cup chopped pecans

1. In a medium saucepan, stir the brown sugar over medium-high heat until melted. Stir in the cream and salt and bring to a boil. Reduce the heat and simmer for about 5 minutes, or until thickened.

2. Remove from the heat to cool slightly, 3 to 5 minutes. Stir in the chopped pecans.

Vegan Salted Caramel Sauce

This sweet-and-salty topping is incidentally vegan, but don't let that stop you from using it on your favorite cake for something a little bit extra!

PREP TIME: 5 minutes ✦ **MAKES:** 1 cup

½ cup canned coconut cream

½ cup light brown sugar
1½ teaspoons cornstarch

1 teaspoon coarse sea salt

1. In a medium saucepan, combine the coconut cream, brown sugar, and cornstarch and stir over medium-high heat until melted. Bring to a boil, then reduce the heat and simmer for about 5 minutes, or until thickened.

2. Remove from the heat to cool slightly, 3 to 5 minutes. Stir in the sea salt.

STORAGE: Will keep in an airtight container in the refrigerator for about 1 week. Stir before use, as it will have thickened considerably.

Lagniappe

The Cajun-French word *lagniappe* means "something extra," so feel free to finish off your glazed or frosted cakes with any of the following toppings to give it that extra bit of flair. This list is just a suggestion as you are only limited by your imagination when it comes to toppings.

- Shaved chocolate
- Candy-coated chocolates
- Cookie crumbles
- Mini chocolate chips
- Freeze-dried fruit
- Fresh fruit
- Toasted nuts
- Toasted coconut
- Sprinkles

Here are some specific winning combinations:

Southern Chocolate Mayo Cake (page 79)	+	Homemade Whipped Cream (page 130)	+	shaved chocolate
Chocolate Sin Cake (page 82)	+	Small-Batch Chocolate Buttercream (page 133)	+	mini chocolate chips
Lagniappe Cake (page 74)	+	Peanut Butter Glaze (page 128)	+	chopped peanut butter cup candies
Minty Chocolate Cake (page 69)	+	Homemade Whipped Cream (page 130)	+	Thin Mint cookie crumbles
Strawberry Milkshake Cake (page 56)	+	Homemade Whipped Cream (page 130)	+	sliced strawberries
Coconut-Lime Cake (page 50)	+	Small-Batch Vanilla Buttercream (page 132)	+	grated lime zest
Gingerbread Cake (page 113)	+	Homemade Whipped Cream (page 130)	+	sugared cranberries
Pumpkin Spice Latte Cake (page 34)	+	Cream Cheese Glaze (page 127)	+	toasted walnuts
Nutty Caramel Cake (page 106)	+	Pecan Caramel Sauce (page 134)	+	toasted coconut

Measurement Conversions

VOLUME EQUIVALENTS	U.S. STANDARD	U.S. STANDARD (OUNCES)	METRIC (APPROXIMATE)
LIQUID	2 tablespoons	1 fl. oz.	30 mL
	¼ cup	2 fl. oz.	60 mL
	½ cup	4 fl. oz.	120 mL
	1 cup	8 fl. oz.	240 mL
	1½ cups	12 fl. oz.	355 mL
	2 cups or 1 pint	16 fl. oz.	475 mL
	4 cups or 1 quart	32 fl. oz.	1 L
	1 gallon	128 fl. oz.	4 L
DRY	⅛ teaspoon	–	0.5 mL
	¼ teaspoon	–	1 mL
	½ teaspoon	–	2 mL
	¾ teaspoon	–	4 mL
	1 teaspoon	–	5 mL
	1 tablespoon	–	15 mL
	¼ cup	–	59 mL
	⅓ cup	–	79 mL
	½ cup	–	118 mL
	⅔ cup	–	156 mL
	¾ cup	–	177 mL
	1 cup	–	235 mL
	2 cups or 1 pint	–	475 mL
	3 cups	–	700 mL
	4 cups or 1 quart	–	1 L
	½ gallon	–	2 L
	1 gallon	–	4 L

OVEN TEMPERATURES

FAHRENHEIT	CELSIUS (APPROXIMATE)
250°F	120°C
300°F	150°C
325°F	165°C
350°F	180°C
375°F	190°C
400°F	200°C
425°F	220°C
450°F	230°C

WEIGHT EQUIVALENTS

U.S. STANDARD	METRIC (APPROXIMATE)
½ ounce	15 g
1 ounce	30 g
2 ounces	60 g
4 ounces	115 g
8 ounces	225 g
12 ounces	340 g
16 ounces or 1 pound	455 g

Index

About the Author

AIMEE BROUSSARD is a southern food writer, recipe developer, and award-winning author who has appeared on QVC, *Rachael Ray*, and the *Taste of Home Cooking School*. She makes her home in Louisiana with her husband, Brian, and gaggle of Cavalier King Charles spaniels. You'll find her sharing recipes with a side of Southern hospitality on her blog, AimeeBroussard.com. This is her third cookbook.

Printed in the USA
CPSIA information can be obtained
at www.ICGtesting.com
LVHW062230130124
768701LV00001B/4

9 781638 786023